Official Information for Requesters

OFFICIAL INFORMATION FOR REQUESTERS

A COMPREHENSIVE GUIDE TO USING THE OIA AND LGOIMA IN NEW ZEALAND

FIRST EDITION

Arie Joe

Self-Published
Wellington, New Zealand

First published 2026

ISBN 978-0-473-78255-9 (paperback)

Typeset in Garamond

CONTENTS

Preface

This book is written for anyone who wishes to obtain information held by government in New Zealand. Whether you are a journalist pursuing an investigation, a researcher gathering data, an advocate seeking accountability, a lawyer advising a client, a business navigating regulation, or simply a citizen who believes the public has a right to know how decisions are made on its behalf, this guide is for you.

New Zealand's Official Information Act 1982 and the Local Government Official Information and Meetings Act 1987 are among the most progressive freedom-of-information statutes in the world. They start from the principle that official information must be made available unless there is good reason to withhold it. That principle, simple as it sounds, represents a profound constitutional commitment.

Yet for all the strength of the legislation, navigating the official information system can be daunting. The Acts are not always straightforward. Agencies do not always respond as they should. Knowing your rights is one thing; knowing how to exercise them effectively is another.

The Office of the Ombudsman publishes excellent guides, and their work is invaluable. But there has long been a gap: a comprehensive, practical reference written from the requester's perspective. This book aims to fill that gap.

A note on terminology: the OIA and LGOIMA are closely related statutes. Where they differ, this book highlights the difference. Otherwise, references to "the Act" should be taken to cover both.

Arie Joe
Wellington, New Zealand, 2026

PART ONE

FOUNDATIONS

CHAPTER 1

The Right to Know: History and Purpose of the OIA

If you are reading this book, you probably want to know how to get information out of a government agency. Before you learn the mechanics of making a request, it is worth understanding why the right to request information exists at all, where it came from, and what it is designed to achieve. The history matters because it shapes how the law works in practice, and because knowing the purposes of the legislation gives you a powerful tool when agencies resist disclosure.

New Zealand before the OIA

For most of the twentieth century, New Zealand had no general right of access to government-held information. The governing statute was the Official Secrets Act 1951, which was modelled on the United Kingdom's Official Secrets Act 1911. The Official Secrets Act was not primarily about managing access to information in an orderly way. It was a criminal statute, designed to prevent the unauthorised disclosure of government information. Its central concern was espionage and the leaking of sensitive material, but its reach was broad enough to cast a shadow over all government information.

Under the Official Secrets Act, the default position was secrecy. There was no presumption that government information should be available to the public, no formal process for requesting access, and no independent body to review refusals. If a public servant chose not to share information, there was little a member of the public could do about it.

This legal framework both reflected and reinforced a culture of closed government. Public servants operated on the assumption that official information belonged to the Crown and was not to be shared unless there was a specific reason to do so. Government departments were under no obligation to explain their decisions, to publish their internal policies, or to account for how they used public resources. Information flowed upwards to Ministers and outwards to Parliament, but the public was largely excluded from this process.

By the mid-1970s, this culture of secrecy was coming under increasing pressure. Freedom of information had become a political issue in New Zealand, as it had in Australia, Canada, and the United States. In 1977, an opposition MP introduced a Freedom of Information Bill, which lapsed after its first reading. Early in 1978, the Public Issues Committee of the Auckland District Law Society published a report recommending that a commission of inquiry or non-partisan parliamentary task force be established to consider the issues and recommend legislative change. Within government, there was a growing recognition that the existing system was no longer sustainable.

The Danks Committee and the Towards Open Government Reports

In May 1978, the government responded by establishing the Committee on Official Information, chaired by Sir Alan Danks, the former chairman of the University Grants Committee. The committee became known as the Danks Committee. Its seven members included representatives from the State Services Commission, the Prime Minister's Department, the Department of Justice, and the Ministries of Defence and Foreign Affairs. Only one other member besides Sir Alan came from outside the public service: Professor (later Sir) Kenneth Keith of the Law Faculty at Victoria University of Wellington.

The predominant public service representation on the committee attracted criticism at the time, but it proved to be an important factor in making the eventual proposals acceptable to both politicians and the bureaucracy. This was a deliberate choice. The committee's terms of reference went beyond reviewing the classification system and the Official Secrets Act. The basic task, as the terms of reference put it, was to contribute to the larger aim of freedom of information by considering the extent to which official information could be made readily available to the public.

The committee received submissions from over 130 individuals and organisations, about half from outside government. It closely followed the freedom of information debates and law reform efforts in Australia and Canada, and studied the schemes adopted in the United States and Sweden. But it was determined to find solutions suited to New Zealand's particular needs and circumstances.

The committee published its General Report, titled *Towards Open Government*, in early 1981. The Supplementary Report followed in July 1981, containing a draft Official Information Bill with detailed annotations. Together, these reports set out a comprehensive case for replacing the culture of secrecy with a presumption of openness, and proposed a legislative framework to give that presumption legal force.

The fundamental change the committee proposed was simple but radical: instead of a default of secrecy, the new regime would start from a default of availability. Information would be released unless there was a good reason to withhold it. The reasons for withholding would be specified in the legislation and described in broad, principled terms rather than rigid categories. An independent review authority (the Ombudsmen) would investigate complaints from requesters who were dissatisfied with the response they received.

Two aspects of the Danks Committee's thinking are worth highlighting, because they remain relevant to how the system operates today.

First, the committee emphasised from the outset that the proposed regime had two goals, not one: to release information and to protect it. These goals were in inherent conflict, and the committee expected that balancing them would always involve difficulty. This is why the legislation is built around a case-by-case assessment of competing interests rather than rigid rules. The committee designed a regime that allowed the balance to be revisited and adjusted over time through practical experience.

Second, the committee was clear that greater release of information was a means to an end, not an end in itself. The OIA was intended to improve the relationship between citizens and the state. As the committee put it, access to official information was part of a wider general issue involving the whole interrelationship of government and the community, and the mutual advantage in communication and cooperation. The test of the success of the regime was not simply whether information was regularly released through the mechanics of the Act, but whether there had been meaningful development in the communication between the people of New Zealand and their government.

The Passage of the Official Information Act 1982

The National Government introduced the Danks Committee's draft Bill into Parliament without alteration, though it reserved the right to make changes. The Bill was referred to a special Parliamentary Select Committee, which heard a large number of submissions, particularly from government departments that had not previously had an opportunity to comment. Some important changes were made at the select committee stage. In particular, Parliament retained the Information Authority (a body proposed by the Danks Committee to oversee the implementation of the new regime) but imposed a sunset clause, meaning the Authority would expire in 1987. The select committee also rewrote the provisions protecting government decision-making processes, attempting to elaborate on and clarify the reasons that might justify withholding information in that context.

The Official Information Act 1982 received Royal Assent on 17 December 1982 and came into force on 1 July 1983. In a remarkably short period, New Zealand had moved from a regime based on criminal sanctions for disclosure to one based on a legal presumption of availability.

The early years of the Act's operation were shaped by the work of the Information Authority, which focused on implementation and on building understanding of the new system within the public service. When the Authority expired in 1987, as the sunset clause required, nothing replaced its function of ongoing regulatory oversight and development. This loss has been a recurring theme in commentary on the Act. The collective corporate memory of the public service on OIA matters has at times faded, and the spirit of the legislation has sometimes been lost to decision-makers who did not experience the cultural shift that the Act was designed to bring about.

The Local Government Official Information and Meetings Act 1987

The OIA as originally enacted applied to central government agencies and Ministers of the Crown. It did not cover local government. That gap was filled by the Local Government Official Information and Meetings Act 1987, commonly known as LGOIMA. LGOIMA was enacted as part of a broader package of amendments that also significantly updated the OIA itself.

LGOIMA applies the same fundamental principles as the OIA to local authorities and council-controlled organisations. The principle of availability is expressed in identical terms. The purposes are substantially the same, adapted to the local government context: instead of promoting accountability of Ministers and officials and enabling participation in the making and administration of laws and policies, LGOIMA promotes accountability of local authority members and officials and enables more effective participation by the public in the actions and decisions of local authorities.

There are, however, some differences between the two Acts. LGOIMA has no eligibility restrictions: anyone can request information from a local authority, regardless of citizenship or residence. LGOIMA also includes provisions governing public access to local authority meetings and agendas, reflecting the additional purpose of promoting the open and public transaction of business at meetings of local authorities. The withholding grounds are substantially the same as those in the OIA, though there are fewer of them (reflecting the different constitutional position of local government).

For the purposes of this book, most of the legal principles discussed apply equally under both Acts. Where there are important differences, they are noted.

The Principle of Availability

The heart of the OIA is section 5, the principle of availability. It provides that where the question of whether any official information is to be made available arises under the Act, that question shall be determined in accordance with the purposes of the Act and the principle that the information shall be made available unless there is good reason for withholding it.

This provision is not merely a preamble or a statement of aspiration. It is a substantive legal rule that governs the interpretation and application of every other provision in the Act. The courts have described the OIA as a constitutional measure, and an important component of New Zealand's constitutional matrix. The Ombudsmen have stressed time and again that the Act must receive a fair, large, and liberal interpretation that best attains its objects as set out in sections 4 and 5.

What the principle of availability means in practice is that the starting point for every request is release, not withholding. When you make a request, the agency must begin from the assumption that it will provide the information. If it wishes to withhold, it bears the burden of identifying a specific ground in the Act that justifies doing so. There is no general power to withhold information because it is inconvenient, embarrassing, politically sensitive, or simply because the agency would prefer not to release it.

This is the single most important thing to understand about the OIA, and it is worth keeping in mind throughout this book. The principle of availability is your strongest argument whenever an agency resists disclosure, and it is the lens through which the Ombudsman assesses every complaint.

The Purposes of the Legislation

Section 4 of the OIA sets out the three purposes of the Act, consistently with the principle of the Executive Government's responsibility to Parliament.

The first purpose is to increase progressively the availability of official information to the people of New Zealand, in order to enable their more effective participation in the making and administration of laws and policies, and to promote the accountability of Ministers of the Crown and officials, and thereby to enhance respect for the law and to promote the good government of New Zealand. This is the most important purpose, and it contains several ideas packed tightly together. The word "progressively" signals that the Danks Committee expected the culture of openness to develop over time, with the scope of available information expanding as the system matured. The reference to participation recognises that democracy requires informed citizens who can engage meaningfully with the decisions that affect them. The reference to accountability reflects the constitutional principle that those who exercise public power must be answerable for how they use it.

The second purpose is to provide for proper access by each person to official information relating to that person. This is the basis for requests for personal information, which are dealt with under Part 4 of the OIA and which intersect with the Privacy Act 2020.

The third purpose is to protect official information to the extent consistent with the public interest and the preservation of personal privacy. This is sometimes overlooked by advocates of transparency, but it is a genuine purpose of the Act. The OIA does not require the indiscriminate release of all government information. It requires a careful balancing of competing interests, with the scales tilted in favour of release but with genuine recognition that some information needs to be protected.

These three purposes work together. They establish that the Act is not a one-way ratchet for disclosure, but a framework for balancing openness against legitimate protection. Understanding this balance is essential for effective use of the Act, because it is the balance that agencies, the Ombudsman, and the courts apply when deciding whether information should be released.

The OIA within New Zealand's Constitutional Framework

The OIA does not operate in isolation. It is one of several statutes that together form the framework for managing government information and ensuring public accountability in New Zealand.

The Ombudsmen Act 1975 provides the institutional machinery for reviewing OIA decisions. The Ombudsmen are Officers of Parliament, independent of the executive, and their role in investigating complaints about OIA decisions is central to the Act's effectiveness. Without the Ombudsmen, the OIA's presumption of availability would be little more than a statement of good intentions. It is the availability of independent review that gives the principle its teeth.

The Privacy Act 2020 (which replaced the Privacy Act 1993) governs the collection, use, storage, and disclosure of personal information by agencies. Where a request under the OIA relates to the requester's own personal information, the request is processed under Part 4 of the OIA, which incorporates the principles of the Privacy Act. The Privacy Act does not limit or affect the operation of the OIA, but the two statutes operate in parallel: the OIA governs access to official information generally, while the Privacy Act focuses specifically on individuals' rights in relation to information about themselves.

The Public Records Act 2005 requires agencies to create and maintain full and accurate records of their affairs. This is the foundation on which the OIA rests, because the OIA can only provide access to information that exists. If agencies do not create or retain records, the right of access is hollow. The Ombudsman has found in a number of cases that agencies cannot rely on their own failures of recordkeeping to justify a response that information is not held.

Together, these statutes create a system in which government agencies are required to create and keep records of their work, the public has a right to access those records, and an independent body can investigate and remedy failures to comply with that right. The system is not perfect, as this book will make clear, but its design is coherent and its principles are sound.

Comparisons with Freedom of Information Regimes in Other Countries

New Zealand's OIA is part of a global movement towards freedom of information that gathered strength in the second half of the twentieth century. The Danks Committee studied the schemes adopted in the United States, Sweden, Australia, and Canada, and drew lessons from all of them while designing a system suited to New Zealand's particular circumstances. A brief comparison helps to highlight what makes the New Zealand model distinctive.

The United States Freedom of Information Act, enacted in 1966, was the pioneer. It created a legally enforceable right of access to federal government records, subject to nine specific exemptions. The US system is characterised by its formality: disputes are resolved by the federal courts, and there is a strong culture of litigation around FOI requests. The US Act applies only to documents (records), not to information more broadly.

Australia enacted its Freedom of Information Act in 1982, the same year as New Zealand. The Australian system shares many features with the New Zealand model, including a presumption of access and a set of exemptions that must be justified case by case. However, the Australian system originally relied on a tribunal (the Administrative Appeals Tribunal) for external review, rather than an Ombudsman, and has undergone significant reform since, including the creation of the Australian Information Commissioner. The Australian Act originally used class-based exemptions (categories of documents that were automatically exempt) alongside harm-based exemptions (which required a showing of prejudice). The New Zealand model, by contrast, is almost entirely harm-based: information can only be withheld if disclosure would cause a specific kind of harm or prejudice.

The United Kingdom did not enact freedom of information legislation until 2000, nearly two decades after New Zealand. The UK Freedom of Information Act 2000 created a right of access to information held by public authorities, with a set of exemptions and a public interest test similar in structure to the New Zealand model. The UK system uses an Information Commissioner as the first-tier review mechanism, with an Information Tribunal for appeals. The UK Act is notably more complex than the New Zealand OIA, with a larger number of exemptions and more elaborate procedural requirements.

Canada enacted its Access to Information Act in 1983, a year after New Zealand. The Canadian system is broadly similar in structure but has been criticised for the breadth of its exemptions and the weakness of its enforcement mechanisms. The Canadian Information Commissioner can make recommendations but cannot order disclosure, a feature shared with the New Zealand Ombudsmen (though in New Zealand, the Ombudsman's recommendations create a legally binding duty to comply unless overridden by Order in Council).

What makes the New Zealand model distinctive? Several features stand out. First, simplicity: the OIA is a short, plainly drafted statute that avoids the complexity and procedural burden of the US and UK systems. Second, breadth: the OIA applies to "information" rather than "documents" or "records," which means that undocumented information known to agency staff can be requested. Third, the use of the Ombudsmen as the primary review mechanism, which keeps the system informal, accessible, free of charge, and non-adversarial, in contrast to the court-based or tribunal-based systems used elsewhere. Fourth, the harm-based approach to exemptions: rather than categorising information into exempt and non-exempt classes, the OIA requires the agency to demonstrate that disclosure would cause a specific kind of harm in the circumstances of the particular case. Fifth, the public interest override: for most withholding grounds, the agency must consider whether the public interest in release outweighs the need to withhold, ensuring that protection is never absolute where the public interest demands disclosure.

The Ongoing Relevance and Reform Debates

The OIA is now more than four decades old, and the environment in which it operates has changed enormously. The volume of government information has grown exponentially with the rise of electronic communications. The political environment has become more contested and media-driven. Proactive release of government information (publishing it without waiting for a request) has become common practice, driven by Cabinet Office requirements and agency policies. Other transparency mechanisms, including the Public Finance Act 1989, the Privacy Act, and the pre-trial criminal disclosure regime, have supplemented the OIA's role.

Despite these changes, the OIA itself has been amended only modestly since 1987. The Law Commission conducted a comprehensive review of the official information legislation, publishing its report *The Public's Right to Know* in 2012 (NZLC R125). The report made a large number of recommendations for reform, including strengthening the Ombudsman's enforcement powers, clarifying the charging framework, improving the provisions for proactive release, and addressing the difficulties posed by electronic information. Many of these recommendations have not been implemented.

Chief Ombudsman Peter Boshier, who served from 2015 to 2025, was a prominent advocate for reform throughout his tenure. The number of OIA complaints received by the Ombudsman's office increased by 110 percent over the course of his time in the role, reflecting both greater public awareness of the OIA and growing frustration with how agencies were administering it.

Commentary on the Act has consistently identified several areas of concern. These include: delay in responding to requests, with the 20-working-day maximum being treated as a target rather than a backstop; the use of withholding grounds (particularly free and frank opinions) in an expansive way that goes beyond what the Danks Committee contemplated; the perception that charging and substantial collation or research are sometimes used as deterrents rather than genuine administrative tools; the tension between departmental decision-making and ministerial involvement in OIA processes; and the absence of any body (since the expiry of the Information Authority in 1987) with responsibility for overseeing the system as a whole and promoting continuous improvement.

At the same time, the Act has been widely recognised as a success. Former Chief Ombudsman Sir Brian Elwood concluded in 1999 that New Zealand had achieved across the total public sector as open a process of governance as any yet devised. The Danks Committee's evolutionary approach has proved remarkably durable. The core principles of the Act, the presumption of availability, the harm-based withholding grounds, the public interest test, and the Ombudsman as independent reviewer, remain sound. The challenges lie not in the design of the legislation but in its administration, and in ensuring that the culture of openness the Act was intended to foster continues to develop as circumstances change.

For requesters, the practical significance of this history is straightforward. The OIA exists because New Zealand made a deliberate choice to move from a culture of secrecy to a culture of openness. The principle of availability is not a vague aspiration but a binding legal rule. When you make a request, the law is on your side. Understanding that, and understanding the purposes the Act is designed to serve, will make you a more effective and more confident requester.

CHAPTER 2

Who Can Request and Who Must Respond

One of the first things you need to know before making a request for official information is whether you are entitled to make one, and whether the body you want to ask is required to respond. This chapter deals with both sides of that equation: who can request, and who must answer.

Eligibility to Make OIA Requests

The OIA does not give every person in the world the right to request information from the New Zealand government. Section 12(1) sets out five categories of person who may make a request:

1. A New Zealand citizen.
2. A permanent resident of New Zealand.
3. A person who is in New Zealand.
4. A body corporate which is incorporated in New Zealand.
5. A body corporate which is incorporated outside New Zealand but which has a place of business here.

These categories are deliberately broad. They cover the vast majority of people who are likely to want to use the Act. If you are a New Zealand citizen living overseas, you are eligible. If you are a tourist visiting the country, you are eligible for as long as you are physically present. If you are a company registered in New Zealand, or a foreign company with a New Zealand office, you are eligible.

The only people effectively excluded are individuals who are outside New Zealand and who are not New Zealand citizens or permanent residents. In practice, this means overseas-based foreigners. Foreign companies without a New Zealand place of business are also excluded.

There is no age restriction. There is no requirement that you have any particular interest in the information, or that you be affected by it. You do not need to give your reasons for wanting the information, and no agency can compel you to do so. You do not need to be a voter, a taxpayer, or a ratepayer. The right is deliberately broad because the OIA's purposes, as discussed in Chapter 1, centre on public participation and government accountability, and these purposes are best served by making the right of access as wide as possible.

An agency is entitled to ask reasonable questions to verify that you meet the eligibility requirements, but this should not be used as a barrier to legitimate requests. In the case of requests made by post, your address may make your eligibility obvious. In the case of online requests, particularly those made through fyi.org.nz, it may be less clear, and the agency may need to make enquiries. These enquiries should be made promptly and should not be used as a delaying tactic.

There is one important carve-out to note. If you are a natural person (that is, an individual human being rather than a company or organisation) and you are requesting personal information about yourself, your request will be treated as having been made under the Privacy Act 2020, not the OIA. This happens automatically by operation of section 12(1A) of the OIA. It does not matter whether you mention the OIA, the Privacy Act, or neither. The legislation directs your request to the right track based on the nature of the information sought and who is seeking it.

No Eligibility Restrictions under LGOIMA

The position under LGOIMA is simpler and more generous. There are no eligibility restrictions at all. Any person, anywhere in the world, may request official information from a local government agency under LGOIMA. You do not need to be a New Zealand citizen or resident. You do not need to be in New Zealand. You do not even need to be a natural person.

This is a significant difference from the OIA, and it means that if you are a person who would not qualify to make a request under the OIA (for example, because you are an overseas-based foreigner), you can still request information from any local authority, council-controlled organisation, or other body subject to the LGOIMA without any restriction.

What to Do If You Are Not Eligible under the OIA

If you do not fall into one of the five categories of eligible requester under the OIA, you are not without options.

First, you can still ask an agency for information informally. While the agency is not required to respond in the terms set out by the OIA (and the statutory time limits and other protections do not apply), it should still deal with your request in a reasonable manner. Many agencies will provide information to ineligible requesters as a matter of good practice.

Second, if the agency you want information from is also subject to the Ombudsmen Act 1975, its handling of your informal request could still be the subject of a complaint to the Ombudsman, not under the OIA, but under the general jurisdiction of the Ombudsmen Act. The Ombudsman can investigate complaints about unreasonable conduct by agencies subject to that Act.

Third, you can use an agent. There is nothing in the OIA that prevents an eligible person from making a request on behalf of someone who is ineligible. If you are an overseas-based foreigner, you could ask a friend, colleague, or lawyer in New Zealand to make the request for you. The only limitation is that the agent-based approach does not work for requests for personal information under Part 4 of the OIA, or for requests for reasons for a decision under section 23. Those rights are personal and cannot be exercised through an agent acting on behalf of someone who does not meet the eligibility requirements.

Fourth, as noted above, you can request information from local government agencies under LGOIMA without any eligibility restriction at all.

Agencies Subject to the OIA

The OIA applies to a wide range of central government bodies. Understanding which bodies are covered, and which are not, is essential to making an effective request.

The types of agencies subject to the OIA include:

Ministers of the Crown, but only in their official capacity. A Minister's private correspondence, electorate-related material held in their capacity as a Member of Parliament, and political party or caucus material are not "official information" and cannot be requested under the OIA. The boundary between a Minister's official and non-official capacities can sometimes be difficult to draw, and agencies (including Ministers themselves) must make this determination on a case-by-case basis. Information can cross from non-official to official if it is used for ministerial purposes.

Government departments and ministries, which are the core of the public service. All departments are subject to the OIA. They are listed in Part 1 of Schedule 1 of the Ombudsmen Act 1975.

Crown entities, which include a diverse range of bodies such as the Accident Compensation Corporation, the Earthquake Commission, the Human Rights Commission, and many others.

State-owned enterprises, at least those that remain listed in the relevant schedules. The question of whether SOEs should be subject to the OIA was debated at the time the State-Owned Enterprises Act 1986 was enacted. Some argued that subjecting SOEs to the OIA put them at a competitive disadvantage relative to private sector businesses. Parliament rejected that argument, and a select committee review in 1989-1990 recommended that SOEs continue to be subject to the legislation. However, as SOEs have been privatised over the years, they have been removed from the schedules and are no longer covered.

Other organisations listed in the schedules, including the Police, Te Whatu Ora (Health New Zealand), universities, polytechnics, wananga and other tertiary education institutions (though not private training establishments), and boards of state schools.

The full list of agencies subject to the OIA can be found in Schedule 1 of the Ombudsmen Act 1975 and Schedule 1 of the OIA itself. A consolidated list is also published in the *Directory of Official Information*, available on the Ministry of Justice website at www.justice.govt.nz.

If you are unsure whether a particular body is subject to the OIA, the Office of the Ombudsman can advise. You can call them on freephone 0800 802 602.

Agencies Subject to LGOIMA

The LGOIMA applies to local government bodies. The types of agencies covered include:

City, district, and regional councils. These are the primary units of local government in New Zealand, and they hold vast quantities of information relevant to the communities they serve: resource consent applications, building consent records, rates information, policy documents, meeting minutes, contracts with service providers, and much more.

Council-controlled organisations (CCOs). These are bodies in which one or more local authorities hold a controlling interest. They include entities such as Auckland Transport, Christchurch City Holdings, and various other organisations that perform functions on behalf of local authorities.

Local and community boards, which are subordinate bodies within the local government structure.

Licensing trusts and airport authorities, which are also subject to the LGOIMA.

The agencies subject to LGOIMA are listed in Schedule 1 of that Act. As with the OIA, if you are unsure whether a particular local government body is covered, the Ombudsman's office can help.

How to Find Out Which Agency Holds Your Information

One of the most common practical challenges for requesters is working out which agency to send your request to. Government is large and complex, and the same topic may involve multiple agencies with overlapping responsibilities. Environmental information, for example, might be held by the Ministry for the Environment, a regional council, a district council, the Environmental Protection Authority, or all of them. Health information might sit with the Ministry of Health, Te Whatu Ora, a district health board (in respect of historical records), or a Crown research institute.

There are several strategies for working out where to direct your request.

Start with the agency's website. Most government agencies have websites that describe their functions, responsibilities, and organisational structure. This will often give you a good indication of whether the agency is likely to hold the kind of information you are looking for.

Use the *Directory of Official Information.* Published by the Ministry of Justice, the Directory lists agencies subject to the OIA along with descriptions of their functions and the types of information they hold. It also lists the contact person within each agency who is responsible for handling OIA requests.

If you are not sure, ask. You can ring an agency and ask whether it holds the kind of information you are seeking. You can also ring the Office of the Ombudsman for guidance.

Do not worry too much about getting it wrong. If you send your request to the wrong agency, the OIA requires that agency to transfer your request to the correct one, provided it believes the information is held by, or more closely connected with the functions of, another agency. The transfer must happen within 10 working days of your request being received. The receiving agency must inform you of the transfer. So while it is better to get it right first time (because transfers add delay), sending your request to the wrong place is not fatal.

One important point: the obligation to transfer applies only to agencies that are subject to the same legislation. An agency subject to the OIA must transfer to another OIA agency (or to a Minister). An agency subject to the LGOIMA must transfer to another LGOIMA agency. Transfers between the two regimes are not provided for in the legislation.

Requests to Ministers versus Requests to Departments

The OIA applies separately to Ministers and to departments. Both are subject to the Act, but they have distinct roles and responsibilities, and the practical implications of directing your request to one rather than the other can be significant. Understanding this distinction is important for any requester who is seeking information about government policy, ministerial decision-making, or the relationship between political and administrative arms of government.

The starting point is that departments and Ministers are independent decision-makers under the OIA. When a department receives a request, it is the department (specifically, the chief executive or their authorised delegate) that must make the decision on it. The Minister does not make the decision, and the department is not required to seek the Minister's approval or clearance.

However, the relationship between departments and Ministers in the OIA context is more complex than this simple rule suggests. Three mechanisms exist for managing the interface.

Transfer. If a department receives a request for information that it does not hold, or that is more closely connected with the functions of the Minister, it must transfer the request to the Minister. This shifts decision-making responsibility to the Minister's office. From your perspective as a requester, a transfer means that the 20 working day clock restarts from the day after the Minister receives the transferred request, which adds delay. Requesters can sometimes be suspicious of transfers to Ministers, perceiving them as a tactic to delay or to shift the decision to someone more likely to withhold. The Ombudsman has made clear that transfers must be based on genuine statutory grounds, and that a department cannot transfer a request simply because the Minister wants to control the response.

Consultation. A department may consult the Minister before making its decision on a request. Unlike transfer, consultation does not shift the decision-making responsibility. The department still makes the decision. Consultation is a discretion, not an obligation, and it should only occur when the department genuinely needs the Minister's input to make a proper decision, for example because the information relates to the Minister's functions or because release could affect the Minister's legitimate interests. The Ombudsman has criticised blanket policies under which departments refer all OIA requests to the Minister's office for comment. Such practices are not contemplated by the Act and can lead to unnecessary delays.

Notification. This is the lightest touch mechanism. A department may simply notify the Minister's office that a particular OIA request has been received and advise the Minister of the decision the department proposes to make, without seeking any input. This is often done under the "no surprises" convention, which the Cabinet Manual describes as an expectation that Ministers will not be surprised by matters that could be the subject of public or political comment. Notification should not delay the department's response.

From a requester's perspective, the practical implication is this: if you want information that a department holds, direct your request to the department. If you want information that the Minister holds (or that is more closely connected with the Minister's functions), direct it to the Minister. If you are not sure, direct it to the department and let it decide whether a transfer is necessary.

Be aware that requests directed to Ministers can sometimes take longer to process than requests directed to departments. Ministers' offices are typically smaller than departmental OIA teams, and the political sensitivity that attaches to ministerial decisions can lead to more cautious (and slower) handling.

Also be aware that what a Minister holds in their "official capacity" is not always straightforward. A Minister may hold information as a Minister, as a Member of Parliament, as a member of a political party, or in a purely private capacity. Only information held in their capacity as a Minister is "official information" subject to the OIA. If you request information and the Minister says it is held only in their capacity as an MP or in a private capacity, you may wish to challenge that characterisation through a complaint to the Ombudsman.

Parliamentary Privilege and the Limits of the OIA

Parliament and its agencies are not subject to the OIA. This is a deliberate exclusion, grounded in the constitutional principle of parliamentary privilege, which protects the proceedings of Parliament from interference by the executive and the courts.

The bodies not covered by the OIA include:

The Parliamentary Service, which provides administrative and support services to Parliament and to Members of Parliament.

The Parliamentary Counsel Office, which drafts legislation.

The Office of the Clerk of the House of Representatives, which provides procedural and administrative services to the House and its committees.

Select committees, which are committees of Members of Parliament that examine legislation, conduct inquiries, and hold the executive to account. Submissions made to select committees, evidence given to them, and their internal deliberations are all protected by parliamentary privilege and are not accessible under the OIA.

This exclusion has practical consequences for requesters. If you want to see the submissions made to a select committee on a particular bill, you cannot use the OIA to get them. (In practice, many submissions are published on the Parliament website, but this is a matter of parliamentary practice, not a legal requirement under the OIA.) If you want to see advice given to a select committee by parliamentary officials, that too falls outside the OIA.

However, there is an important distinction to draw. Information that relates to parliamentary proceedings but is held by an agency subject to the OIA (such as a government department) may still be accessible under the OIA, subject to the withholding grounds. For example, a department's briefing to a Minister in preparation for a select committee appearance is held by the department in its official capacity and is, in principle, official information. Whether it can be released will depend on whether any withholding grounds apply, including section 18(c)(ii) (which allows refusal if release would constitute contempt of the House) and section 9(2)(g)(i) (free and frank opinions).

The Parliamentary Privileges Act 2014 codifies the law of parliamentary privilege in New Zealand. It protects "proceedings in Parliament" from being questioned or impeached in any court or place outside Parliament. The Ombudsman has published guidance on the intersection of the OIA and parliamentary privilege, which provides a useful framework for understanding when information can and cannot be withheld on these grounds.

Bodies Not Covered by the OIA or LGOIMA

Several categories of bodies fall outside both the OIA and the LGOIMA entirely.

Courts and tribunals are not subject to the OIA in their judicial capacity. This reflects the constitutional principle of judicial independence. You cannot use the OIA to obtain a court's deliberations, its draft judgments, or its internal working documents. However, court decisions are generally public documents, and many are published online through the Ministry of Justice and other databases. Administrative information held by the Ministry of Justice about the courts (as distinct from information held by the courts in their judicial capacity) may be accessible under the OIA.

The Ombudsman is not subject to the OIA. This is perhaps unsurprising, given the Ombudsman's role as the independent reviewer of OIA decisions. Correspondence between agencies and the Ombudsman in relation to investigations is specifically excluded from the definition of "official information."

The Independent Police Conduct Authority is similarly not subject to the OIA.

The intelligence and security agencies present a more nuanced picture. The New Zealand Security Intelligence Service (NZSIS) and the Government Communications Security Bureau (GCSB) are subject to the OIA, but in practice the conclusive withholding grounds in section 6 (particularly those relating to security, defence, and the maintenance of the law) will apply to much of the information they hold. Requests to these agencies are possible, but the scope of what can be released is significantly constrained.

Private entities are not subject to the OIA or LGOIMA. This means that private companies, non-governmental organisations, charities, and individuals acting in a private capacity are not required to release information under the official information legislation, no matter how significant the information might be. The boundary between public and private has become increasingly important as government has contracted out many functions to private providers. If a private company holds information that was generated in the course of performing a government contract, you will generally need to request it from the government agency that let the contract, not from the private company itself.

The process of corporatisation and privatisation over the past four decades has also affected coverage. When a state-owned enterprise is privatised and sold to the private sector, it is removed from the schedules to the OIA and ceases to be covered. Several former SOEs have been removed in this way. Some privatisation statutes include transitional provisions ensuring that complaints already received by the Ombudsman, or investigations already under way, are not affected by the removal. But once the transition is complete, the body is no longer subject to the Act.

The Danks Committee, when it designed the OIA, flagged the possibility that coverage might be extended to Parliament and its associated organisations in the future. That has not happened. Successive commentators have argued for such an extension, and it remains a live question in discussions about reform of the official information legislation. For now, however, the exclusions described above remain in place.

Understanding the boundaries of coverage is an essential first step in making an effective request. If the body you want information from is not subject to the OIA or LGOIMA, you will need to find alternative avenues, whether that means requesting the information from a different agency that is covered, using other legislation (such as the Privacy Act), or relying on informal channels.

CHAPTER 3

What Is "Official Information"?

The scope of what you can request under the OIA depends on two things: what counts as "official information," and what counts as "held." These concepts are broader than most people expect, and understanding them is one of the keys to making effective requests. This chapter explains the statutory definition, explores its reach, identifies the boundaries, and introduces three special categories of information to which you have enhanced rights of access.

The Statutory Definition

The OIA does not define "official information" by listing types of documents. Instead, it uses a deliberately expansive formulation. Under section 2 of the OIA, "official information" means any information held by a department, a Minister of the Crown (in their official capacity), or an organisation subject to the Act.

Under the LGOIMA, the definition is even simpler: "official information" means any information held by a local authority.

The critical word in both definitions is "information," not "document." This is one of the most important features of the New Zealand legislation, and one that distinguishes it from freedom of information laws in many other countries. The OIA is not a right of access to documents. It is a right of access to information. This distinction has profound practical consequences.

The Breadth of the Definition

Because the right is to information rather than to documents, the scope of what you can request is very wide. Official information includes, but is not limited to:

Written documents of every kind: reports, memos, letters, notes, emails, text messages, instant messages, draft documents, briefings, Cabinet papers, ministerial submissions, internal policy papers, meeting minutes, file notes, and correspondence.

Non-written documentary material: information stored on or generated by computers and databases, video and audio recordings, photographs, maps, plans, graphs, drawings, spreadsheets, presentations, and any other material recorded or stored by means of any device.

Metadata: information about information, such as the date a document was created or modified, who created it, who it was sent to, and what search terms were used to locate it. Metadata can be just as revealing as the documents it describes, and it falls within the definition of official information.

Undocumented information: information that is known to people within an agency but has not yet been recorded in writing or in any other form. If an official has knowledge of a matter in their official capacity, that knowledge is official information, even if it has never been written down. The agency may need to reduce it to writing in order to respond to your request, but this does not amount to the "creation" of new information. It is simply the provision of existing information in a different form.

Data held in electronic databases: information that can be extracted from a database by running a query or search. Even if the specific output you are requesting has never been generated before, the underlying data is held by the agency, and extracting it by running a query is collation of existing information, not the creation of something new.

The definition also extends to information held outside New Zealand by any branch or post of a department or organisation. If a New Zealand government agency has an overseas office, the information held by that office is official information.

What the definition does not cover is information that does not yet exist and would need to be created through the application of complex skill, judgement, or interpretation. There is a distinction between collating existing information (which agencies must do) and creating new information (which they are not required to do). If answering your request would require the agency to form an opinion, generate an analysis, or construct something fundamentally new from raw material, that goes beyond what the OIA requires. But if the task is simply to compile, extract, or present information that is already held in some form, the agency cannot refuse on the basis that the specific compilation does not already exist.

Information "Held" by an Agency

The concept of "held" is the second critical element of the definition. It determines whether information falls within the OIA's reach.

"Held" is not limited to information that is physically in the agency's possession. The OIA contains several "deeming provisions" that extend the concept of "held" to include information that is in the control of the agency, even if it is physically located elsewhere. The Ombudsman has said that the question of whether information is held should be interpreted as broadly as possible.

Notions of information "ownership" or "intellectual property" are not relevant. The fact that a third party may hold copyright in information does not affect its status as information "held" by an agency, nor is it a reason, in and of itself, to withhold it.

Information held by employees

Information held by an officer, employee, or member of an agency in their official capacity is deemed to be held by the agency itself. This is a deeming provision in section 2(4) of the OIA, and it has several important implications.

First, it covers information held in the minds of employees that has not been written down. If an official knows something in their official capacity, that knowledge is official information. The information must be "known" to the individual (meaning it is clear, certain, or established) and able to be recalled. Obviously, the more recent the information, the more likely it can be recalled. On request, the agency should reduce unrecorded information to writing and release it, unless there is a good reason for withholding.

Second, it covers information held on employees' personal devices or personal email accounts, provided the information was generated, communicated, received, or otherwise held in the employee's official capacity. The Ombudsman has been clear on this point: the use of private email accounts or personal devices does not override the application of the official information legislation. In one case, the Ombudsman required a regional councillor to produce emails from his private email account because they had been sent in his official capacity as a councillor. In another case, the New Zealand Defence Force was deemed to hold battle footage recorded by soldiers on their personal devices, because the footage was recorded in the soldiers' official capacity.

Third, the deeming provision applies only to current officers, employees, or members, not to former ones. Once a person ceases to be an employee of an agency, information in their personal possession is no longer deemed to be held by the agency.

Fourth, it does not include information that an employee holds only in their private capacity. Information that an official knows purely as a private citizen, unconnected to their role, is not official information. The boundary between official and private capacity is determined by considering the nature and content of the information, the context in which it came to be held, the role and functions of the employee, how the information relates to that role, and any use to which the information has been put. Information can cross from private to official if it is used for official purposes.

Information held by independent contractors

Where an agency engages an independent contractor, any information held by the contractor in their capacity as contractor to the agency is deemed to be held by the agency. This deeming provision, in section 2(5) of the OIA, ensures that agencies cannot avoid the OIA by contracting out functions to the private sector.

If the information is not in the agency's physical possession because it is held only by the contractor, the agency will need to take steps to obtain it in order to comply with its obligations under the OIA. The Ombudsman has recommended that agencies include standard terms and conditions in their contracts for services that enable them to access official information held by contractors.

The deeming provision applies only to information held by the contractor in their capacity as contractor. Information the contractor holds in some other capacity (for example, as part of their general business operations unrelated to the government contract) is not deemed to be held by the agency.

Information held by unincorporated bodies set up by agencies

Under section 2(2) and (3) of the OIA, where an unincorporated body (however described) is established by legislation, or by a department, Minister, or organisation, in order to assist, advise, or perform functions connected with that agency, any information held by the unincorporated body is deemed to be held by the agency that established it.
This covers advisory boards, working groups, committees, task forces, panels, and any other entities that an agency creates to assist with its work, where those entities do not have their own separate legal personality. If, for example, a government department sets up an expert advisory panel to report on a policy question, and that panel is not itself subject to the OIA, the information held by the panel is nevertheless deemed to be held by the department.

What Is Not Official Information

Despite the breadth of the definition, certain categories of information are specifically excluded. Even if an agency physically holds this information, it is not "official information" for the purposes of the OIA, and it cannot be requested under the Act.
The exclusions under the OIA are:

Library or museum material held solely for reference or exhibition purposes. This prevents the OIA from being used as a means of accessing library collections or museum exhibits. The exclusion applies only where the material is held "solely" for these purposes. If the material is also used for other purposes (for example, as a source for policy advice), it may still be official information.

Information held solely as an agent or for the sole purpose of safe custody on behalf of a person not subject to the OIA. This prevents information that happens to be in government storage, but belongs to a private party, from becoming accessible simply by virtue of the storage arrangement. For this exclusion to apply, there should be evidence that the agency is acting solely as the other person's agent, or that the information is held for no purpose other than safe custody. If the agency uses the information, or is entitled to use it, the exclusion will not apply.

Information held by the Public Trustee or Maori Trustee in their capacity as a trustee. This protects private trust information from disclosure.

Evidence or submissions to a Royal Commission or a commission of inquiry. This recognises the distinct legal framework governing inquiries.
Certain information related to inquiries established under the Inquiries Act 2013.

Correspondence or communication between any agency and the Ombudsman or the Privacy Commissioner, in relation to their investigations. This protects the confidentiality of the investigation process.

Victim impact statements.

Certain information provided to the Judicial Conduct Commissioner, a Judicial Conduct Panel, or the Judicial Complaints Lay Observer.

Under the LGOIMA, the exclusions for library and museum material, safe custody material, and Inquiries Act material also apply, along with the others that are relevant to the local government context.
If an agency refuses your request on the basis that the information falls within one of these exclusions, it will typically rely on section 18(g) of the OIA (section 17(g) of the LGOIMA), which allows refusal where the information is not held. If you disagree, you can complain to the Ombudsman.

Information Held by Ministers

As discussed in Chapter 2, Ministers are subject to the OIA, but only information they hold in their official capacity as Ministers is "official information." Information held by a Minister in their private capacity, in their capacity as a Member of Parliament (electorate material), or in their capacity as a member of a political party (caucus material) is not official information and cannot be requested under the Act.

Determining which capacity applies can be contentious. The Ombudsman has identified the following factors to consider: the nature and content of the information, the context in which it came to be held, and the use to which it has been put. Information can become official if it is used for ministerial purposes, even if it was originally received in a non-official capacity.

When a Minister leaves office, they are no longer subject to the OIA. Information that was held by former Ministers may still be accessible if it is held by a current Minister or by a department. Ministers leaving office are required to return all internal departmental material to the originating department. Remaining ministerial papers may be deposited at Archives New Zealand, subject to agreed conditions, or destroyed securely.

The Distinction between Official Information and Personal Information

One of the most common sources of confusion for requesters is the boundary between the OIA and the Privacy Act 2020. The two statutes operate in parallel, and the same file or database may contain information governed by both.

The basic rule is straightforward. If you are a natural person (an individual human being) requesting information about yourself, your request is governed by the Privacy Act, not the OIA. This happens automatically. Section 12(1A) of the OIA provides that a request by or on behalf of a natural person for access to personal information about that person is deemed to be a request under the Privacy Act, and the OIA does not apply.

If you are requesting information about someone else, or about a topic that happens to include information about other people, the OIA (or LGOIMA) applies. The agency will then need to consider whether any withholding grounds apply to protect the privacy of the individuals concerned (under section 9(2)(a) of the OIA, for example).

In practice, many files contain a mix of information about the requester and information about other people. When this happens, the agency must split the request. Information solely about the requester is considered under the Privacy Act. Information about other people is considered under the OIA or LGOIMA.

When the Privacy Act applies instead

The Privacy Act gives individuals a right to access personal information about themselves held by any agency (not just government agencies, but also private sector organisations). The right is broader in scope than the OIA in this respect. Complaints about refusals to provide personal information under the

Privacy Act are made to the Privacy Commissioner, not the Ombudsman. The contact details for the Office of the Privacy Commissioner are:

Phone: 0800 803 909 Email: enquiries@privacy.org.nz Website: www.privacy.org.nz

Acting as an agent for someone else's personal information

If you are seeking personal information on behalf of another person with their informed consent, you will generally be considered to be acting as that person's agent. In this case, the request will be dealt with as a request for personal information under the Privacy Act, not the OIA.

It is worth being clear in your request about whether you are acting as an agent. If the agency is uncertain, it may need to verify the authority of the agent, and this can cause delay.

Special Categories of Information with Enhanced Rights of Access

The OIA and LGOIMA create enhanced rights of access to three particular categories of information. These are not just ordinary requests with a different label. They carry specific statutory rights, and the grounds on which the agency can refuse are more limited than for ordinary Part 2 requests. If your situation falls within one of these categories, it is worth knowing about the enhanced right and invoking it explicitly.

Internal rules and guidelines for decision making (section 22 OIA / section 21 LGOIMA)

You have a right to access any document held by an agency that contains policies, principles, rules, or guidelines in accordance with which decisions or recommendations are made about people in their personal capacity. This is the right created by section 22 of the OIA (section 21 of the LGOIMA).

The word "document" here is broad. It includes manuals, handbooks, policy guides, standard operating procedures, assessment criteria, scoring rubrics, checklists, and any other document that guides decision-making about individuals. The key requirement is that the document must be used in making decisions or recommendations about people in their personal capacity. It does not need to be in the form of a formal direction or even advice. It is the manner of use, not outward form, that determines whether section 22 applies. Collations of precedent in the form of summaries of past decisions will qualify if they are used to guide future conduct.

The decision or recommendation need not affect you personally. It is sufficient that it affects any person or group in their personal capacity. You do not need to be the subject of the decision to exercise the right.

Common examples include: immigration instructions and policy manuals, benefit eligibility criteria, prosecution guidelines, police operational procedures, school enrolment policies, grant assessment criteria, and human resources policies used for recruitment, promotion, or disciplinary decisions.

The grounds on which such a request can be refused are significantly more limited than for ordinary requests. Several of the commonly invoked withholding grounds, notably free and frank opinions (section 9(2)(g)(i)) and legal professional privilege (section 9(2)(h)), cannot be used to refuse a section 22 request. Agencies should not expect to be able to withhold information on these grounds.

There is no special form required for a section 22 request. You can make it orally or in writing, and you do not need to refer to section 22. However, it helps to do so, because it alerts the agency to the fact that the enhanced right applies and that the usual range of withholding grounds is not available.

Statements of reasons for decisions (section 23 OIA / section 22 LGOIMA)

If an agency has made a decision or recommendation about you in your personal capacity, you have a right to request a written statement of the reasons for that decision or recommendation. This is the right created by section 23 of the OIA (section 22 of the LGOIMA).

The statement of reasons must include three elements: the findings on material issues of fact; a reference to the information on which those findings were based (subject to limited exceptions); and the reasons for the decision or recommendation.

This is a powerful right that is often underused. It goes beyond simply requesting the documents in the agency's file. Even if the agency holds very little documented information about the decision, it must still provide a written statement explaining the reasoning. The statement should be full and comprehensive. It is not enough for the agency to point you to previous correspondence or to say that it has already explained its reasons informally.

The request must be made within a "reasonable time" of the decision or recommendation. What is reasonable will depend on the circumstances, but you should not wait indefinitely. Make your request as soon as you become aware of the decision you want explained.

As with section 22 requests, the grounds for refusal are more limited than for ordinary requests. Free and frank opinions and legal professional privilege cannot be used to refuse. Where legal advice has been adopted and relied on in reaching a decision, information about the reasons for doing so must still be supplied.

It is a good idea to refer specifically to section 23 when making your request, so there can be no doubt about the nature of the right you are invoking. However, it is not strictly required. If it is reasonably clear from the terms of your request that you are seeking the reasons for a decision about you, the agency should recognise it as a section 23 request and process it accordingly.

Note the distinction between a request for reasons (which engages section 23 and its enhanced right) and a general request for information relating to a decision (which is an ordinary Part 2 request). To trigger section 23, you must be seeking the reasons why a decision was made about you, not simply requesting copies of all documents on the file.

Personal information requests by corporate entities (Part 4)

Under Part 4 of the OIA and LGOIMA, a corporate entity (that is, a company or incorporated society, not a natural person) can request the personal information that an agency holds about it. This is the corporate equivalent of the individual's right under the Privacy Act.

Under the OIA, this right can only be exercised by corporate entities that are incorporated in New Zealand or have a place of business here. Under LGOIMA, the right can be exercised by any corporate entity, regardless of where it is incorporated.

The requirements for processing Part 4 requests are broadly the same as for ordinary requests, but the grounds for refusal are more limited. In particular, free and frank opinions (section 9(2)(g)(i)) cannot be used to refuse a Part 4 request. This is significant, because it means that agencies cannot withhold information about a corporate entity on the basis that release would inhibit free and frank advice in the future.

A Part 4 request may look like an ordinary OIA or LGOIMA request. What sets it apart is the nature of the requester (a corporate entity rather than an individual) and the nature of the information sought (information about the requester itself). If you are a corporate entity making a request for information about your organisation, it is worth mentioning Part 4 in your request to ensure that the agency applies the correct (and more favourable) refusal grounds.

Practical Implications for Requesters

Understanding what counts as official information, and what "held" means, can make a real difference to the effectiveness of your requests.

If you suspect that relevant information exists on employees' personal devices or email accounts, say so in your request. Agencies are obliged to search for and produce information held in their official capacity on personal devices, but they may not do so proactively unless you raise the issue.

If you are interested in information held by contractors, ask the agency about it. The agency may need to obtain the information from the contractor, and it helps if the agency knows from the outset that this is likely to be necessary.

If your situation involves a decision about you personally, consider whether a section 23 request for reasons might serve you better than a general request for documents. The section 23 right requires the agency to explain its reasoning, even if the documented record is thin.

If you are a company or incorporated society, be aware of your enhanced rights under Part 4. You have a right to access information about your organisation, and the grounds on which the agency can refuse are narrower than for ordinary requests.

And if you are told that the information you want is "not held," do not accept this at face value without understanding what the agency has searched for and why. The Ombudsman's guidance makes clear that agencies must make reasonable efforts to locate information, and that the deeming provisions extend the concept of "held" well beyond what is physically sitting in the agency's filing cabinets.

PART TWO

MAKING YOUR REQUEST

CHAPTER 4

Before You Request: Research and Strategy

The best OIA requests are not written on impulse. They are the product of preparation: knowing what is already public, understanding how the agency works, thinking carefully about what you actually need, and planning how to get it. The time you invest before you send your request will pay for itself many times over in faster responses, lower charges, fewer refusals, and better results.

This chapter is about the work that happens before you write a single word of your request.

Starting with What Is Already Publicly Available

Before you ask a government agency for information, check whether it is already public. This sounds obvious, but it is remarkable how often people make OIA requests for information that is freely available on the internet. Agencies notice this too, and while they are required to respond to your request regardless, starting with what is already out there will help you target your OIA requests at the information that is genuinely not public, which is where the Act adds the most value.

There are several places to look.

Agency websites. Most government departments and Crown entities publish a significant amount of information on their websites: annual reports, statements of intent, corporate strategies, consultation documents, regulatory guidance, policy papers, statistical reports, media releases, and much more. Many agencies also publish their organisational structure, the names and roles of senior staff, and contact details for their OIA team. Start here.

Proactive releases. Over the past decade, a growing culture of proactive release has transformed the amount of official information that is published without being asked for. Cabinet Office requirements now call for the proactive release of Cabinet papers and related material, usually within 30 business days of decisions being taken. Many agencies proactively publish briefings to incoming Ministers, advice to Ministers on significant policy issues, and responses to OIA requests. Some agencies maintain "disclosure logs" where they publish OIA responses as a matter of course. Look for a "proactive release" or "OIA responses" section on the agency's website.

The fyi.org.nz archive. FYI (short for "Free Your Information") is a website that allows anyone to make OIA and LGOIMA requests online. All requests and responses are automatically published on the site, creating a searchable public archive of OIA correspondence. Before making your own request, search FYI to see whether someone has already asked for similar information. You may find that the information you want has already been released, or you may learn something about how the agency handles requests on your topic that helps you frame your own request more effectively. Even if the earlier request was refused, the agency's reasons for refusal can be instructive: they tell you which withholding grounds the agency is likely to rely on, and may help you design a request that avoids those grounds.

Government data portals. The government publishes a wide range of datasets on data.govt.nz, which is the central portal for open government data. Budget information is available on budget.govt.nz. Tender and procurement information is available on gets.govt.nz (the Government Electronic Tenders Service). Crime statistics are published on policedata.nz. Health data, education data, environmental data, and many other categories of information are published by the agencies responsible for those areas. If what you need is statistical or data-based, check the relevant data portals before making an OIA request.

The beehive.govt.nz website. This is the official website of the New Zealand Government and includes ministerial press releases, speeches, and (since 2018) proactively released ministerial diaries.

Parliamentary and select committee publications. Hansard (the record of parliamentary debates), select committee reports, submissions on bills (where published), and written parliamentary questions and answers are all available through the New Zealand Parliament website at parliament.nz.

Ombudsman case notes and opinions. The Office of the Ombudsman publishes case notes and opinions on its website at ombudsman.parliament.nz. If you are interested in how the OIA has been applied to a particular type of information, searching the Ombudsman's published case notes can give you valuable insight into the likely outcome of a request, and the arguments that may carry weight.

The point of this preliminary research is not to avoid using the OIA. It is to use the OIA more effectively. The information you find in the public domain will help you understand the landscape, identify the gaps, and frame requests that are targeted, specific, and difficult to refuse.

Understanding How Government Agencies Are Structured

Government agencies are not monolithic. They are complex organisations with internal divisions, branches, teams, and units, each with its own area of responsibility. Understanding how an agency is structured can help you identify where the information you want is likely to be held, and it can help you frame your request in terms that the agency's staff will recognise and be able to act on.

Most agencies publish their organisational structure on their website, often in the form of an organisational chart. This will show you the senior leadership team and the major divisions beneath them. Some agencies go further and publish the names and contact details of team leaders and managers at lower levels.

Pay attention to the way the agency divides up its work. A large department like the Ministry of Education, for example, will have separate divisions responsible for policy, operations, data and analytics, legal services, finance, and corporate functions. If you are seeking information about a particular policy initiative, the policy division is the most likely holder. If you are seeking financial information, the finance team is where you should look. If you are seeking correspondence between the agency and a particular external party, it may be held by the operational team that manages that relationship, or by the legal team if the correspondence is of a legal nature.

Understanding the structure also helps you anticipate how your request will be processed. In most agencies, OIA requests are received by a central coordination team (often part of the corporate or ministerial services division), which logs the request, assigns it to the relevant business unit, and manages the process through to completion. The coordination team will often consult multiple business units if the request spans more than one area. Knowing this can help you understand why some requests take longer than others, and it can help you engage constructively if the agency comes back to you with questions about the scope of your request.

Identifying the Right Agency

Chapter 2 discussed the range of agencies subject to the OIA and LGOIMA, and gave some advice on how to identify which agency holds the information you are seeking. This section adds some further practical guidance.

The most common mistake is to direct a request to the wrong level of government. Central government departments (covered by the OIA) and local authorities (covered by LGOIMA) hold different types of information, even on the same topic. Resource consents, for example, are granted by local authorities, so the consent files will be held by the relevant council. But the Ministry for the Environment will hold information about the national policy framework within which resource consents are granted. If you are interested in a specific consent decision, the council is the right target. If you are interested in the policy behind the consent framework, the Ministry is the right target. If you want both, you will need to make separate requests to each.

Another common mistake is directing a request to the Minister when the information is held by the department, or vice versa. As discussed in Chapter 2, departments and Ministers are separate decision-makers under the OIA, and directing your request to the wrong one can result in a transfer that adds delay. If you want operational or administrative information, direct your request to the department. If you want information about ministerial decision-making, direct it to the Minister. If you are unsure, the department is usually the safer choice, because it can transfer to the Minister if necessary.

If you genuinely do not know which agency holds the information, consider making a preliminary phone call or email to ask. Most agencies have a general enquiries line, and their staff can usually tell you quickly whether the agency is the right one or point you in a better direction. You can also call the Office of the Ombudsman for guidance (freephone 0800 802 602).

Remember that if you send your request to the wrong agency, it is required to transfer the request to the right one. This adds up to 10 working days of delay (because the clock restarts after a transfer), but it means that a misdirected request is not wasted. The agency must tell you that it has transferred the request, and to whom.

Thinking about What You Actually Need

This is perhaps the most important part of the preparation process, and the area where requesters most often go wrong. The classic OIA request asks for "all papers, drafts, letters, memos, emails, notes of telephone conversations, and other documents" on a given topic. This kind of request is sometimes necessary, but it is almost always a sign that the requester has not thought carefully enough about what they actually need.

Broad, catch-all requests carry significant risks. The agency may need to extend the time limit because of the volume of information involved. You may be charged for the labour of collation and supply. You may end up with hundreds of pages of material, most of which is irrelevant to your actual concern. In the worst case, your request may be refused entirely under section 18(f) because the information cannot be made available without substantial collation or research.

The better approach is to start by asking yourself: what do I actually want to know? Not what documents do I want to see, but what question am I trying to answer? Once you are clear on the question, you can think about what information would answer it, and then frame your request around that information.

Some practical techniques for narrowing your scope:

Specify a date range. Instead of asking for all correspondence on a topic, ask for correspondence within a defined period. This reduces the volume significantly and makes the agency's search task more manageable.

Specify the type of information. If you are interested in the policy advice that was given to a Minister, ask for briefings, aide-memoires, and Cabinet papers, rather than for "all documents." If you are interested in the cost of a project, ask for financial reports and invoices, not for "all records relating to" the project.

Exclude what you do not need. If you are not interested in internal emails, draft documents, or personal information about individuals, say so in your request. This reduces the work the agency has to do (and the charges it may impose on you), and it reduces the risk of a refusal on the grounds of substantial collation or research.

Be clear about the subject matter. The more precisely you can describe the topic, the easier it is for the agency to identify the relevant information. Instead of asking for "all documents about housing policy," ask for "the briefing to the Minister on the proposed changes to the Residential Tenancies Act that were announced in March 2025."

There is, however, a countervailing risk in being too narrow. If you specify your request so tightly that it misses relevant information held in an unexpected place or under an unexpected label, you will not receive it. The agency is only required to respond to the request you have made, not to the request you might have made if you had known more about how the information was organised. Striking the right balance between too broad and too narrow is a matter of judgement, and it improves with experience.

If you are uncertain about the right scope, consider making a preliminary inquiry. You can call the agency and ask, in general terms, what kind of information it holds on your topic. This is not an OIA request, and the agency is not obliged to answer, but most will. The information you gain from this preliminary conversation can help you frame a much more effective OIA request.

Developing a Requesting Strategy for Complex Investigations

If you are using the OIA for something more than a single, standalone question, it pays to think strategically about how to sequence and coordinate your requests.

Start with the overview, then drill down. For a complex topic, consider beginning with a broad, high-level request designed to give you a picture of the landscape: what key documents exist, what decisions have been made, who was involved. This might be a request for the table of contents of a file, the titles and dates of all briefings on a topic within a particular period, or a summary of the key decisions made. Once you have this overview, you can make targeted follow-up requests for the specific documents that interest you most. This two-stage approach is often more effective (and cheaper) than a single broad request for everything.

Sequence your requests to build on each other. Each response you receive will teach you something about how the agency organises its information and what it holds. Use this knowledge to inform subsequent requests. The first response may reveal the existence of a report you did not know about, or the involvement of another agency you had not considered. Your second request can be more targeted as a result.

Make cross-agency requests where appropriate. Many government activities involve multiple agencies. A policy initiative may be led by one department but involve input from several others, as well as consultation with Ministers, external advisors, and affected parties. If you want a complete picture, you may need to make parallel requests to multiple agencies. Be aware that each agency will process its request independently, and that responses may arrive at different times and in different formats. Keeping track of what you have requested from whom, and what you have received, becomes important.

Use proactive releases and FYI responses as leads. The information you find in the public domain can point you toward information that is not yet public. A proactively released Cabinet paper may refer to a piece of advice from an agency that has not been released. An FYI response may mention the existence of a report that you can then request in full. Treat publicly available information as a starting point for further inquiry, not as the end of the trail.

Consider the timing of your requests. If an issue is politically sensitive or publicly contentious, agencies may handle requests more cautiously, and the involvement of Ministers' offices through consultation or notification may add delay. If timeliness is important to you, consider making your request as early as possible, and consider requesting urgency (with reasons) if there is a genuine basis for it. On the other hand, if the issue is not time-critical, you may get a better result by waiting until the immediate political heat has passed, when the agency may feel less pressure to withhold.

Think about the format of the information you want. If you are requesting data, ask for it in a reusable electronic format (such as a spreadsheet or CSV file) rather than a PDF or printed document. The agency is required to provide information in the format you prefer, unless there is a good reason not to. Receiving data in a reusable format saves you the work of retyping or re-entering it.

Keeping Records of Your Research and Planning

Finally, keep records of everything. This advice applies to the preliminary research phase, the requests themselves, and the responses you receive.

Keep a log of the publicly available information you have found and where you found it, so that you can refer back to it without repeating the search. Note the URLs and the dates you accessed them, as government websites change over time and information may be moved or removed.

Keep copies of every request you send, including the date, the agency, the method of communication (email, letter, FYI, phone), and the name of the person you sent it to or spoke with. If you make an oral request, write down what you asked for, when, how, and who you spoke to. This record will be essential if the agency loses your request, fails to respond within the statutory time limit, or disputes the scope of what you asked for.

Keep copies of every response you receive, and note the date of receipt. If you receive information in multiple instalments, note which parts were received when. This becomes important if you later need to complain to the Ombudsman about delays or incomplete responses.

If the agency contacts you to discuss your request, whether to seek clarification, to suggest a narrower scope, or to advise you of a charge, keep a record of the conversation. Note the date, who you spoke with, what was discussed, and what was agreed. Follow up in writing to confirm the key points. A clear record of these interactions can be invaluable if a dispute arises later.

For complex investigations involving multiple requests to multiple agencies over an extended period, consider maintaining a simple tracking spreadsheet. Record each request, the agency, the date sent, the date acknowledged, any extensions or charges notified, the date of the response, and a summary of what was received. This will help you stay on top of your requests and identify patterns, such as agencies that consistently respond late, or topics where withholding grounds are repeatedly invoked.

Good records are not just an administrative discipline. They are the foundation of effective use of the OIA. If you ever need to complain to the Ombudsman, you will need to be able to show what you requested, when, and what happened. The better your records, the stronger your position.

CHAPTER 5

Crafting an Effective Request

Chapter 4 was about preparation. This chapter is about execution: how to write a request that is clear, specific, and effective. A well-crafted request is one that the agency can understand, act on, and respond to without unnecessary delay, charges, or confusion. It is also one that gives you the best chance of getting the information you actually need.

The Basics

Making an OIA request is, in law, remarkably simple. Section 12(1AA) of the OIA provides that a request may be made "in any form and communicated by any means (including orally)" and "does not need to refer to this Act." The same applies under LGOIMA.

This means:

You do not need to use legal language. Plain English is not only acceptable but preferable. A request that says "please provide a copy of the briefing to the Minister on the proposed changes to the Residential Tenancies Act, dated around March 2025" is perfectly good. You do not need to cite section numbers, use formal salutations, or adopt a legalistic tone.

You do not need to cite the OIA or LGOIMA. The agency is required to recognise a request for official information regardless of whether you mention the legislation. In practice, however, it is helpful to say that you are making a request under the OIA (or LGOIMA), because this helps the person who receives your request to identify it quickly and route it to the right team. It also removes any ambiguity about whether you are making a casual inquiry or a formal request that triggers the statutory time limits and obligations.

You do not need to put your request in writing. You can make a request in person or over the phone. However, putting your request in writing is strongly recommended. A written request creates a clear record of what you asked for and when, which is invaluable if a dispute arises later about the scope of the request, the date it was received, or whether the agency responded within the statutory time limit. If you do make an oral request, the agency may ask you to put it in writing for clarification. If you are unable or unwilling to do so, the agency must make a written record of its understanding of your request and provide you with a copy. Your request will not be treated as "received" until you confirm that the agency's record is correct, which means the 20 working day clock will not start until that confirmation is given.

You do not need to give reasons for wanting the information. The OIA does not require you to explain why you want the information or what you intend to do with it. An agency can ask for your reasons, but it cannot insist that they be supplied.

The Duty of Due Particularity

The one formal requirement that the OIA does impose on you as a requester is that the information you are seeking must be "specified with due particularity." This is the language of section 12(2) of the OIA (section 10(2) of the LGOIMA), and it simply means that the agency must be able to identify the information you have asked for. The person receiving your request must be able to understand what you want.

Due particularity does not mean you have to know the exact title of a document, or the precise file number, or the name of the official who wrote it. It means you have to provide enough detail for the agency to work out what information you are seeking and go and find it. If the agency cannot understand your request, it has a duty to provide you with reasonable assistance to help you clarify it. Reasonable assistance means more than simply telling you that your request is not specific enough. The agency should actively help you to formulate a request it can work with.

A request that lacks due particularity will not be treated as a valid request, and the statutory time limits will not begin to run until the request has been clarified. This is one reason why it pays to be as clear as possible from the outset. Every exchange of clarification adds time.

It is important to understand what due particularity does not require. It does not prevent you from asking for a lot of information. A request for "all briefings from the Ministry of Health to the Minister of Health on the Covid-19 vaccination programme between 1 January 2024 and 30 June 2024" is both broad and entirely specific. The agency knows exactly what it is looking for, even if the volume of material is large. Due particularity is about clarity, not about volume.

How to Describe the Information You Want

There are several ways to frame your request, and the best approach will depend on what you are looking for. You can describe the information by reference to any combination of the following:

Topic or subject matter. This is the most common approach. You describe the subject you are interested in and ask for the information the agency holds on it. For example: "all information held by the Ministry of Education relating to the proposed changes to school zoning rules announced in February 2025." When using this approach, be as precise as you can about the topic. The more specific your description, the easier it is for the agency to identify the relevant material.

Document type. If you know what kind of document you are looking for, say so. For example: "all Cabinet papers, ministerial briefings, and aide-memoires relating to the proposed changes to school zoning rules." Specifying document types helps the agency narrow its search and reduces the risk of being overwhelmed with material you do not need, such as routine internal emails or administrative records.

Date range. Specifying a date range is one of the most effective ways to manage the scope of your request. Instead of asking for everything on a topic since the beginning of time, ask for information created or received within a defined period. For example: "briefings to the Minister on this topic between 1 March 2025 and 31 May 2025." If the topic spans a long period, consider breaking it into phases and making separate requests for each.

Author or recipient. If you know that the information was created by or sent to a particular person or team, you can use that to narrow the search. For example: "correspondence between the Chief Executive of the Ministry and the Secretary to the Treasury regarding the proposed policy, between January and March 2025."

Function or decision. If your interest is in a particular decision or process, frame your request around that. For example: "all information considered by the Minister in making the decision to approve the grant to [organisation], including the application, any assessment reports, the Minister's briefing, and the decision letter."

You can combine these approaches. A request that specifies a topic, a document type, a date range, and a function is far easier for the agency to act on than one that simply asks for "all documents relating to" a subject.

When (and When Not) to Explain Why You Want the Information

The law does not require you to give reasons, and many experienced requesters choose not to, on the principle that the OIA creates a right of access that does not depend on the requester's motivation.

There are, however, situations where providing reasons can work to your advantage.

If the agency needs to apply the public interest test (because a withholding ground under section 9 is engaged), your reasons for wanting the information can help the agency assess whether the public interest in release outweighs the need to withhold. For example, if you are a journalist investigating a matter of significant public concern, saying so may strengthen the public interest case for release. If you are a researcher working on a project that will contribute to public understanding of an important policy issue, explaining this may have a similar effect.

If the agency is struggling to identify what you are looking for, providing context about why you want the information can help the agency understand what you are after and direct its search more effectively.

On the other hand, there are situations where providing reasons may not help and could even hurt. If your reasons are personal or commercial, the agency might (rightly or wrongly) view the request less sympathetically. If you are an opposition political researcher, identifying yourself as such may trigger greater political sensitivity in the agency's handling of the request. In some cases, keeping your reasons to yourself is the prudent course.

The key point is that it is always your choice. No agency can compel you to give reasons, and no agency can refuse your request because you have declined to provide them.

Common Mistakes That Lead to Delays, Charges, or Refusals

Requests that are too broad

The classic example is "all documents, emails, memos, letters, notes, draft documents, and file notes relating to [topic]." This kind of catch-all request is almost always a mistake. The agency will need to search across multiple teams and systems, review a potentially enormous volume of material, make withholding decisions on each document, and prepare the information for release. The likely outcomes include extended timeframes, charges for the labour involved, or an outright refusal under section 18(f) on the grounds that the information cannot be made available without substantial collation or research.

The better approach, as discussed in Chapter 4, is to think about what you actually need and frame your request around that. If you genuinely need everything on a topic, consider breaking the request into stages: start with a request for a list or summary of the key documents, and then make follow-up requests for the specific items that interest you.

Requests that are too narrow

The opposite problem is less commonly discussed but equally real. If you frame your request so narrowly that it describes only part of what the agency holds, you will receive only that part. The agency is not required to go beyond the scope of your request and volunteer additional information that you did not ask for, even if it is clearly relevant.

For example, if you ask for "the Minister's briefing on the proposed changes to school zoning," you will receive that briefing, but you may miss the accompanying aide-memoire, the Cabinet paper that followed, and the departmental report that informed the briefing. If you had asked for "all advice to the Minister relating to the proposed changes to school zoning, including briefings, aide-memoires, Cabinet papers, and supporting reports," you would have captured the full picture.

The risk of being too narrow is greatest when you do not know how the agency organises its information or what types of documents it produces. The preliminary research discussed in Chapter 4 can help reduce this risk.

Requests that inadvertently ask for information that does not exist

Sometimes a request is framed in a way that assumes the agency holds information in a particular form when it does not. For example, you might ask for "the agency's report on [topic]" when no such report exists, even though the agency holds extensive information on the topic in other forms, such as internal emails, file notes, and briefings.

If the specific document you have asked for does not exist, the agency may simply refuse under section 18(e) (the document alleged to contain the information does not exist) or section 18(g) (the information is not held). You will then need to reformulate your request.

To avoid this problem, consider framing your request in terms of the information you want rather than the specific document you think it is in. Instead of asking for "the report," ask for "all information held by the agency on [topic], including but not limited to reports, briefings, correspondence, and file notes."

Specifying the Format You Want the Information In

You have the right to specify how you would like the information to be provided. The agency is required to make the information available in the way you prefer, unless there is a good reason not to (for example, because providing it in that format would impair the efficient administration of the agency).

Common format options include: copies of documents (electronic or hard copy), inspection of the original records at the agency's offices, an oral briefing, a summary or excerpt, or data in a reusable electronic format such as a spreadsheet or CSV file.

If you do not specify a format, the agency will choose one for you, and it may not be the most useful. If you are requesting data, always ask for it in a reusable electronic format. If you want to be able to search, sort, and analyse the information, a PDF or printed document is far less useful than a spreadsheet or database export.

If the agency decides not to provide the information in the way you prefer, it must explain the reasons for that decision. If you disagree, you can complain to the Ombudsman.

It is also worth mentioning that you can indicate you are happy to receive the information in an alternative form if it would make things easier for the agency. For example, you might say: "I would prefer to receive copies of the documents, but I am also happy to inspect them at your offices if that is more convenient." This kind of flexibility can help build a constructive relationship with the agency's OIA team and may result in a faster response.

Requesting Urgency

If you need the information urgently, you can ask the agency to treat your request as urgent. Section 12(3) of the OIA requires that if you request urgency, you must give your reasons for seeking the information urgently.

Requesting urgency does not change the statutory time limits. The agency is still required to make and communicate its decision within 20 working days (or such extended period as may apply). What urgency does is invite the agency to give your request priority over other requests and its existing work. Whether it does so is a matter of judgement, taking into account the reasons you have given, the nature and volume of the information requested, and the agency's other obligations.

Good reasons for urgency include an imminent deadline that depends on the information (for example, a submission deadline, a court hearing, or a publication date), a time-sensitive public interest in the information (for example, a matter currently before Parliament or in the media), or a personal urgency (for example, a decision affecting you that is about to be implemented).

Weak reasons for urgency, such as general impatience or a desire to have the information sooner rather than later, are unlikely to persuade the agency to prioritise your request. Be specific about why you need the information by a particular date, and state that date clearly.

Even if the agency declines to treat your request as urgent, it must still respond within the statutory time limits.

Multiple Requests: Prioritising and Managing a Portfolio

If you are making more than one request, whether to the same agency or to different agencies, it pays to think about how they fit together and how to manage them as a group.

Prioritise. If you are making multiple requests to the same agency, tell the agency which one is most important to you. This helps the agency allocate its resources and may result in the most important information reaching you sooner. Without a stated priority, the agency will process your requests in whatever order suits its workflow, which may not be your preferred order.

Stagger your requests. Sending a large number of requests to the same agency on the same day can overwhelm the agency's OIA team, trigger concerns about frivolous or vexatious behaviour, and create administrative difficulties. If you have multiple requests for the same agency, consider spacing them out over days or weeks. This is not a legal requirement, but it is a practical strategy that tends to produce better results.

Keep a tracking record. As discussed in Chapter 4, maintain a log of every request you have made: the agency, the date sent, what you asked for, the date the response is due, any extensions or charges notified, and the date and content of the response received. For a small number of requests, a simple list will do. For a larger programme of requests, a spreadsheet is essential.

Be prepared to engage. Agencies will sometimes come back to you to discuss the scope of your request, suggest a narrower formulation, or advise you that a charge will be imposed. Treat these interactions as an opportunity, not an obstacle. A constructive dialogue with the agency's OIA team can lead to better outcomes for everyone. If the agency suggests a way of meeting your request that is different from what you originally envisaged, consider whether it would serve your purposes before rejecting it out of hand.

Follow up if you do not hear back. Many agencies will acknowledge your request within a few days. If you do not receive an acknowledgement within a reasonable period (a week is a fair benchmark), follow up. Your request may have gone astray, been overlooked, or been directed to the wrong person within the agency. Early follow-up can save weeks of delay.

CHAPTER 6

Where and How to Send Your Request

You have done your research, identified the right agency, and crafted a clear and specific request. Now you need to deliver it. The channel you choose for sending your request, and the care you take in documenting what you have done, can make a real difference to how smoothly the process runs.

Identifying the Right Person or Team within the Agency

Chapter 4 discussed how to identify the right agency. This section is about finding the right door within that agency.

Most government departments and Crown entities have a dedicated team or person responsible for receiving and coordinating OIA requests. This team may sit within the corporate services division, the ministerial services unit, the governance team, or a standalone official information team. Some agencies have a dedicated OIA email address (such as oiarequest@agency.govt.nz or official.information@agency.govt.nz). Others route requests through their general enquiries address.

Check the agency's website first. Many agencies publish their OIA contact details, sometimes on a dedicated "official information" or "OIA requests" page, sometimes in their "contact us" section. If you cannot find specific OIA contact details on the website, ring the agency's main reception number and ask who handles official information requests.

If you are still unsure, address your request to the chief executive of the agency. You can also write "Request for official information" or "OIA request" in the subject line of your email or the heading of your letter. This signals clearly what your communication is, and reduces the risk that it will be treated as ordinary correspondence and lost in the general mailstream.

Sending your request to the right person or team speeds things up. A request that arrives directly at the OIA coordination point will be logged, assigned, and actioned immediately. A request that arrives at a generic inbox, or on the desk of someone who does not handle OIA requests, may take days or longer to find its way to the right place. Those days count against the 20 working day time limit.

For local authorities under LGOIMA, the position is similar. Most councils have a person or team responsible for official information requests, and their contact details can usually be found on the council's website.

Sending Requests by Email, Letter, In Person, or over the Phone

The OIA allows requests to be made in any form and communicated by any means. In practice, the four main channels are email, letter, in person, and by phone.

Email is the most common and generally the most effective method. It creates an automatic written record of what you asked for and when you sent it. It reaches the agency almost instantly, and the date and time of sending are captured in the email metadata. Most agencies process email requests more quickly than paper requests, because they can be forwarded internally, logged in tracking systems, and responded to electronically without any need for printing, scanning, or physical handling.

When sending by email, use the agency's dedicated OIA email address if one exists. If not, send it to the agency's general enquiries address and clearly mark the subject line as an OIA or LGOIMA request. Attach any supporting material (such as copies of earlier correspondence that provide context for your request) as electronic documents rather than pasting long text into the body of the email.

Letter is still a valid method, though it is slower. A posted letter will take one or more days to reach the agency, and the agency's mail handling process may add further delay before the letter reaches the OIA team. The 20 working day clock starts on the day after the request is received by the agency, not on the day you post it. If timeliness matters, email is preferable.

If you do send a letter, address it to the chief executive or to the OIA contact person (if you have identified one). Put "Request for official information" or "OIA/LGOIMA request" prominently in the heading. Keep a copy of the letter, and note the date you posted it.

In person requests are less common but entirely valid. You can walk into a government agency's office and make a request verbally, or hand-deliver a written request. If you hand-deliver a written request, ask the reception staff to date-stamp your copy or provide a receipt confirming the date of delivery.

Phone requests are possible but carry significant risks, which are discussed in the next section.

Making Oral Requests: What Happens and the Risks Involved

You have the legal right to make an OIA request orally, whether in person or over the phone. Many simple requests can be handled this way without difficulty. But oral requests carry risks that you should understand before relying on them.

The first risk is miscommunication. When you put a request in writing, the agency has a clear and unambiguous record of exactly what you asked for. When you make an oral request, the agency's understanding of what you asked for depends on the accuracy of the person who heard it and recorded it. Misunderstandings are more likely, and if there is a dispute later about the scope of the request, you will have no written record to fall back on.

The second risk is delay. If the agency considers that written clarification of your oral request is reasonably necessary, it is entitled to ask you to put the request in writing. If you are unable or unwilling to do so, the agency must make a written record of its understanding of your request and provide you with a copy. Crucially, your request will not be treated as "received" until you have confirmed that the agency's written record is correct. This means the 20 working day clock does not start until you have given that confirmation. The back-and-forth involved in this process can add days or weeks of delay before the clock even begins.

The third risk is the absence of a paper trail. If the agency fails to respond, or responds late, and you want to complain to the Ombudsman, you will need to show what you requested and when. With a written request, this is straightforward. With an oral request, it depends on your own records.

If you do make an oral request, protect yourself by making a contemporaneous note of what you asked for, when, how (phone or in person), and who you spoke to at the agency. Follow up the oral request with a written confirmation by email, restating what you asked for and noting the date of the original oral request. This gives you a record and gives the agency a clear written reference point.

As a general rule, putting your request in writing is almost always the better choice.

Making Requests through fyi.org.nz

FYI (fyi.org.nz) is a website run by Open New Zealand that allows anyone to make OIA and LGOIMA requests online. It has become one of the most popular channels for making requests, and it has significant advantages. It also has some features and limitations that you should understand before using it.

How it works

You select the agency you want to request information from (FYI maintains a list of "public authorities"), write your request, and submit it through the site. FYI sends the request by email to the agency on your behalf. The agency's response, when it arrives, is also published on the site. All correspondence between you and the agency, including any follow-up questions, extensions, or clarifications, is published as part of the public record.

The benefits

FYI creates a complete, timestamped, publicly accessible record of your request and the agency's response. This is valuable for transparency and accountability. It means you always have proof of what you asked for and when, and the agency knows that its response will be publicly visible, which may encourage a more careful and timely reply.

The FYI archive is searchable, so other people can find and read the responses to your requests. This contributes to the broader pool of publicly available official information. It also means you can search for and learn from other people's requests and responses before making your own.

FYI is free to use and requires no special knowledge or expertise. The interface walks you through the process step by step.

The drawbacks

Automatic publication. The most important thing to understand about FYI is that everything is published. Your request, the agency's response, and all correspondence in between are automatically made available on the website for anyone to read. FYI's policy is not to delete requests, as the site operates as a permanent public archive.

This has several implications. If your request reveals something about your personal circumstances or interests that you would prefer to keep private, FYI is not the right channel. If you are requesting information that might include personal information about you (for example, if you are asking about a decision that affected you), the agency's response may need to address your personal information, and the automatic publication feature creates a risk that personal details could be made public inadvertently. Requesters who want to make their request in private should contact the relevant agency directly rather than using FYI.

The automatic publication feature can also affect how agencies handle your request. Agencies may be more cautious about releasing information that relates to their staff (names, contact details, email addresses) when they know the response will be published online. If you are not seeking staff names or contact details, consider saying so in your request. This may reduce the agency's concerns and lead to a faster response.

Privacy implications for third parties. Because FYI responses are automatically published, agencies will need to think carefully about the privacy implications of releasing information that relates to third parties. This may lead to more redactions than you would receive if you had made the same request directly by email. It may also lead to delays if the agency decides it needs to consult third parties before responding.

Eligibility challenges. When you make a request through FYI, the agency receives your name and a computer-generated @requests.fyi.org.nz email address. Under the OIA (though not LGOIMA), the agency may need to verify that you meet the eligibility requirements. Your FYI profile may not provide enough information for the agency to confirm your eligibility, which can lead to delays while the agency makes enquiries. To reduce this risk, consider including a brief statement of your eligibility in your request (for example: "I am a New Zealand citizen and am eligible to make this request under the OIA").

Email delivery issues. Sometimes FYI does not have the correct email address for an agency, particularly after a change of government, a Cabinet reshuffle (which changes ministerial email addresses), or an agency merger or rebranding. Spam filters can also intercept FYI emails. If you do not receive an acknowledgement within a week, follow up with the agency directly to confirm that your request was received.

When to use FYI and when not to

FYI is an excellent choice for requests on matters of general public interest where you are comfortable with full transparency. It is less suitable for requests that involve personal information about you or others, requests where you want to keep the subject of your inquiry confidential, or requests that require ongoing back-and-forth dialogue with the agency about the scope and framing of the request (because all of that dialogue will be published too).

Making Requests via Social Media

It is legally possible to make an OIA or LGOIMA request via social media, including Twitter (now X), Facebook, and other platforms. The Ombudsman has confirmed that agencies cannot decline to accept a request simply because it was made through social media. In one case, a council that told a requester it could not accept LGOIMA requests over Twitter was found by the Ombudsman to have acted incorrectly.

However, social media is generally not a practical channel for making OIA requests, for several reasons.

Character limits and formatting constraints. Twitter's character limit makes it difficult to frame a request with the specificity and detail that effective requesting requires. You cannot attach documents or provide the kind of context that helps an agency identify the information you are seeking.

Uncertainty about receipt. The 20 working day clock starts when the request is "received" by the agency. For electronic communications sent to an information system that the agency has designated for receiving communications, the request is received when it enters the system. But many agency social media accounts are used for disseminating information, not for receiving it. If the account is not designated for receiving communications, the request is not "received" until it comes to the attention of the agency, and there may be a significant gap between when you post it and when someone notices it.

Requests to Ministers via social media are even more complicated. Ministers may have multiple social media accounts, and it may not be clear whether a particular account is operated in the Minister's official capacity (subject to the OIA), in their capacity as an MP, or in their capacity as a member of a political party. This ambiguity can create uncertainty about whether the request has been validly made and when it was received.

Public visibility. Like FYI, social media requests are visible to anyone. Unlike FYI, there is no structured archive or tracking system, and the request can easily be lost in the flow of posts and comments.

If you do make a request via social media, the Ombudsman recommends invoking the OIA or LGOIMA explicitly, to minimise the risk that your request will be overlooked. You should also request an acknowledgement, and follow up using an alternative method (such as email or phone) if one is not received. Better yet, consider copying your request to an established intake channel of the agency (such as their official email address) at the same time, to ensure it is received.

In most cases, email or FYI will be a more reliable and effective channel than social media.

Keeping Copies and Records of Everything

This point has been made in earlier chapters but bears repeating, because it is the single most important piece of practical advice in this book.

Keep a copy of every request you send. If you send it by email, the sent email is your record. If you send it by letter, keep a photocopy or scan. If you hand-deliver it, get a date-stamped receipt. If you make it through FYI, the site keeps the record for you. If you make an oral request, write down what you asked for, when you asked, who you spoke to, and what they said, and follow up in writing.

Keep a copy of every response you receive, and note the date of receipt. Keep copies of any interim correspondence: acknowledgements, requests for clarification, extension notices, charge notifications, and any emails or phone conversations about the scope of your request.

If you are making multiple requests, maintain a tracking log. A simple spreadsheet works well, with columns for the agency name, the date sent, a brief description of the request, the date any acknowledgement was received, the statutory deadline (20 working days from receipt), any extensions notified, the date the response was received, and a brief note of the outcome.

These records serve three purposes. They help you manage your own requests and stay on top of deadlines. They provide the evidence you need if you want to complain to the Ombudsman. And they form the basis of any follow-up requests you may want to make, because the agency's response (including any reasons given for withholding information) will inform how you frame your next request.

Following Up If You Do Not Receive an Acknowledgement

The OIA does not require agencies to acknowledge receipt of your request. Many agencies do, as a matter of good practice, usually within a few working days. But some do not, and the absence of an acknowledgement does not mean your request has been received or that the clock is ticking.

If you have not received an acknowledgement within about a week of sending your request, follow up. A brief email or phone call is sufficient. Ask the agency to confirm that it has received your request and to advise when you can expect a response.

There are several reasons why an acknowledgement might not arrive. Your request may have gone to the wrong email address and is sitting unread in a general inbox. It may have been caught by a spam filter. It may have been received but not yet assigned to the OIA team. In the case of FYI requests, the email address FYI has on file for the agency may be out of date. In the case of posted letters, the letter may still be in the mail, or it may have been lost.

Early follow-up can prevent small problems from becoming large ones. A request that was lost or misdirected in the first week can still be processed within 20 working days if the problem is caught early. A request that is not discovered until week three, because nobody followed up, is almost certainly going to be late.

When you follow up, keep a record of the follow-up communication as well: who you contacted, when, and what they said. If the agency confirms that it did not receive your request, send it again (or send a copy) and ask the agency to confirm receipt. The 20 working day clock will start from the day after the agency receives the request, whether that is the original or the resent copy.

If the agency confirms that it received your request but has not acknowledged it, ask when you can expect a response. This puts the agency on notice that you are tracking the request and that you expect it to be dealt with within the statutory time limits.

A pattern of constructive, timely follow-up signals to the agency that you are an engaged and organised requester. This tends to produce better results than silence followed by a complaint.

PART THREE

WHAT HAPPENS AFTER YOU REQUEST

CHAPTER 7

The Agency's Process

Understanding how agencies handle OIA requests from the inside is one of the most useful things a requester can know. It will not change your legal rights, but it will change your expectations, your patience, and your ability to engage constructively with the process. It will also help you recognise when something has gone wrong and give you the vocabulary to complain effectively if it has.

This chapter lifts the lid on what happens after your request arrives at the agency's door.

How Agencies Typically Receive and Log Your Request

In most government departments and larger Crown entities, OIA requests follow a standardised workflow. Your request arrives (usually by email) and is received by a central coordination point. In many agencies this is a team within the ministerial and parliamentary services function, the governance and accountability team, or a dedicated official information unit. Some agencies have a shared inbox specifically for OIA requests.

The coordination team logs the request into a tracking system. This system records the date of receipt, the identity of the requester, a brief description of what is being asked for, and the statutory deadline (20 working days from the day after receipt). The request is then assigned to one or more business units within the agency, depending on the subject matter.

In smaller agencies, and in many local authorities, the process may be less formalised. A single person may be responsible for receiving, processing, and responding to all OIA requests. In some very small agencies, the chief executive may handle requests personally.

The coordination team typically manages the process from start to finish: chasing business units for their input, coordinating any internal or external consultation, assembling the draft response, obtaining sign-off from the appropriate decision-maker, and sending the final response to you. In a well-functioning agency, this process is tracked closely, with regular check-ins to ensure the statutory deadline is met.

From your perspective as a requester, the key practical point is this: the sooner your request reaches the coordination team, the sooner the clock starts and the process begins. Sending your request to the right email address (as discussed in Chapter 6) saves the time that would otherwise be lost while your request is forwarded internally from wherever it landed to the team that will actually process it.

Scoping and Interpreting the Request

Once the coordination team receives your request, its first task is to "scope" it: to work out what information you are asking for and what would be involved in providing it.

Scoping means interpreting your request and identifying the information it captures. This involves reading the request carefully, identifying any ambiguity or uncertainty, and making judgements about what falls within and outside the scope of what you have asked for.

If your request is clear and specific, scoping is straightforward. If your request is broad or ambiguous, the agency faces a choice. It can interpret the request in the way it considers most reasonable and proceed on that basis (provided it tells you what interpretation it has adopted, so you can clarify or adjust if needed). Alternatively, it can come back to you and ask for clarification.

If the agency seeks clarification within seven working days of receiving your original request, any amended or clarified version you provide will be treated as a new request, and the 20 working day clock will restart from the day after the new request is received. If the agency waits longer than seven working days before seeking clarification, the clock continues to run from the date the original request was received. This gives agencies an incentive to identify problems with scope early, and it gives you an incentive to respond promptly to any clarification request.

Good scoping involves consulting key staff across the agency to identify where relevant information might be held, interrogating email and document management systems with appropriate search terms to estimate the volume of material, and sometimes conducting a sample review to understand the scale of the task. Agencies that scope properly at the start are far better placed to manage the request efficiently, to engage constructively with you about the scope if needed, and to meet the statutory deadline.

From your perspective, the scoping stage is the most important moment for constructive engagement with the agency. If the agency contacts you to discuss the scope of your request, treat this as an opportunity, not an obstacle. A conversation at this stage can save weeks of processing time and produce a much more useful result than a rigid insistence on the original wording of your request.

The Search for Information

Once the scope is settled, the agency must search its records to find the information that falls within it.

In modern agencies, this typically involves searching electronic document management systems, email systems, shared drives, databases, and sometimes physical filing cabinets or offsite storage. The search is usually conducted by the business unit that holds the information, with guidance from the coordination team about what to look for.

Searches can fail for several reasons. The search terms may not capture all relevant material, particularly if different parts of the agency use different terminology for the same thing. Information may be held on personal devices or in personal email accounts (which, as discussed in Chapter 3, the agency is deemed to hold if the information was generated or received in an official capacity). Filing systems may be incomplete or poorly maintained. Staff turnover may mean that the people who created or received the information are no longer with the agency, and institutional knowledge about where it is stored may have been lost.

The Ombudsman expects agencies to make reasonable efforts to locate information. If an agency tells you it does not hold the information you have requested, and you have reason to believe it should, you can ask what searches were conducted, what systems were checked, and what staff were consulted. If you are not satisfied with the agency's explanation, you can complain to the Ombudsman, who has the power to require agencies to provide a detailed account of their search efforts.

Agencies are not required to conduct perfect searches. But they are required to conduct reasonable ones, using appropriate search terms, checking the systems and locations where the information is likely to be found, and consulting staff who may have knowledge of the information.

Consultation with Third Parties

Before making a decision on your request, an agency may need to consult people or organisations whose interests could be affected by the release of the information. Third party consultation is permitted under the OIA, but it is not required as a matter of routine. It is a discretion that should be exercised when there is a genuine need to obtain the third party's views or to forewarn them of the possibility of release.

The most common scenarios in which third party consultation occurs are:

When the information contains personal information about identifiable individuals (other than you), and the agency needs to assess whether releasing it would be necessary to protect their privacy under section 9(2)(a).

When the information was supplied by a third party in confidence, or contains commercially sensitive material about a third party, and the agency needs to assess whether a withholding ground under section 9(2)(b) or 9(2)(ba) applies.

When the information was supplied by an external organisation (such as a company that provided information as part of a procurement process), and the agency wants to understand the third party's perspective before deciding whether to release it.

From your perspective, the important things to know about third party consultation are as follows.

It takes time. The agency must write to the third party, explain the situation, and give them a reasonable period to respond. If the third party does not respond, the agency must follow up. If the third party objects to release, the agency must consider their views before making its decision. All of this can take weeks, and the agency is entitled to extend the statutory time limit if the consultations cannot be completed within 20 working days.

The third party does not have a veto. Their views are relevant, but not determinative. The agency must reach its own decision on the proper application of the withholding grounds and, where relevant, the countervailing public interest in release. The Ombudsman has been clear on this point: a third party cannot prevent the release of information by simply objecting to it.

The agency should tell you if consultation is necessary. Good practice is for the agency to write to you, let you know that third party consultation is required, and advise you of any extension to the time limit. This gives you an opportunity to say whether you actually need the information about the third party, which may simplify the consultation process or make it unnecessary.

If the information your request captures includes material about third parties that you do not need, consider saying so up front in your request. This can significantly reduce the need for third party consultation and speed up the response.

Consultation with Ministers

As discussed in Chapter 2, the relationship between departments and Ministers in the OIA context involves three mechanisms: transfer, consultation, and notification. This section focuses on consultation and notification, which are the mechanisms most likely to affect how your request is handled.

Consultation occurs when a department seeks the Minister's comment before making its decision on a request. The Act permits this, and it is appropriate when the department genuinely needs the Minister's input, for example because the information relates to the Minister's functions, was supplied by the Minister, or because release could affect the Minister's legitimate interests.

Consultation is a discretion, not an obligation. The Ombudsman has criticised blanket policies under which departments routinely refer all OIA requests to the Minister's office, and has made clear that consultation should be decided on a case-by-case basis. The department must consider the Minister's comments in good faith and with an open mind, but the decision ultimately rests with the department. The Minister's office cannot direct the department to withhold information.

Notification is a lighter process. The department simply advises the Minister's office of the decision it has made (or is about to make) on a request, so that the Minister can prepare for any public or political commentary. This is done under the "no surprises" convention described in the Cabinet Manual, which expects agencies to inform Ministers promptly of matters of significance within their portfolio responsibilities.

Notification is not about seeking clearance or approval. The Ombudsman has stated that seeking ministerial sign-off on OIA responses would be an abdication of the agency's responsibilities under the Act. The decision is the agency's to make, "free from dictation or other improper influence."

From your perspective, the practical impact of ministerial consultation and notification is primarily one of time. If the department consults the Minister, this can add days or weeks to the processing time, and the agency may extend the statutory deadline to accommodate the consultation. If the department merely notifies the Minister, this should not cause significant delay, because notification occurs after the decision has been made.

If you suspect that your request is being delayed because of ministerial involvement, and the agency has not extended the time limit or communicated with you about the reason for the delay, you can follow up with the agency and ask for an explanation. If the statutory deadline passes without a response, you can complain to the Ombudsman, who will investigate whether the delay was justified.

The Decision-Making Process

Once the information has been found, any necessary consultations completed, and the withholding grounds considered, someone within the agency must make the decision on your request.

In government departments, the OIA requires that the decision be made by the chief executive or a person authorised by the chief executive to make the decision. In practice, decision-making authority is usually delegated to senior managers or directors, with particularly sensitive or high-profile requests escalated to the deputy chief executive or chief executive.

The decision must address three questions: whether the request is to be granted (in whole or in part); in what manner the information will be made available (for example, by providing copies, by allowing inspection, or by providing a summary); and whether a charge will be imposed.

If the agency decides to withhold any information, it must identify the specific withholding ground it is relying on and, for the grounds in section 9, apply the public interest test to determine whether the interest in withholding is outweighed by the public interest in release. The agency must communicate the reason for any refusal to you, and must provide the grounds in support of that reason if you ask.

The decision-making process often involves input from multiple parts of the agency: the business unit that holds the information, the legal team (particularly for complex withholding decisions), the communications team (particularly for politically sensitive requests), and the OIA coordination team. In some agencies, the draft response goes through several rounds of review and revision before it is finalised. This internal process is one of the main reasons why responses sometimes take close to the full 20 working days, even for requests that might seem straightforward from the outside.

How Agencies Handle Requests Involving Both OIA and Privacy Act Information

As discussed in Chapter 3, the same file or database may contain information governed by both the OIA and the Privacy Act. When your request captures such a mix, the agency must split the information and apply the correct legal framework to each part.

Information about you (the requester), if you are a natural person, is dealt with under the Privacy Act. Information about other people is dealt with under the OIA or LGOIMA. The agency must consider each part separately and apply the relevant tests. The privacy of other individuals is typically protected under the OIA by section 9(2)(a), which allows withholding where it is necessary to protect the privacy of natural persons. But this is subject to the public interest test, and the agency must consider whether the public interest in release outweighs the need to protect privacy.

In practice, this often means that information about you is released (because the Privacy Act gives you a right of access to your own personal information, subject to limited exceptions), while information about other people in the same documents may be redacted under the OIA's privacy withholding ground.

If you receive a response that applies the Privacy Act to some information and the OIA to the rest, and you are unhappy with the result, you may need to complain to two different bodies: the Privacy Commissioner for the Privacy Act component, and the Ombudsman for the OIA component. This is one of the awkward consequences of having two parallel regimes, and it is worth being aware of at the outset so that you can direct your complaint to the right place.

The Role of OIA Teams, Legal Advisors, and Senior Officials

Understanding who is involved in processing your request can help you understand why decisions are made the way they are, and where problems are most likely to arise.

The OIA coordination team is the engine room. This team receives the request, logs it, assigns it, tracks it through the process, chases overdue inputs from business units, assembles the draft response, manages consultations, and ensures the response is sent before the deadline. The quality and efficiency of this team has a significant impact on how well the agency handles OIA requests. In agencies where the coordination team is well-resourced and experienced, the process tends to run smoothly. In agencies where the team is understaffed or undertrained, delays and errors are more common.

The business unit that holds the information is responsible for conducting the search, identifying the relevant material, and providing initial advice on whether any withholding grounds apply. The business unit staff are typically the people who know the information best, but they may not have deep expertise in the OIA itself. Their instinct may be to withhold more than is legally justified, because they are close to the information and may be sensitive about its release. The coordination team and legal advisors provide a check on this instinct.

Legal advisors are involved in more complex requests, particularly those involving difficult withholding decisions, legally privileged material, commercially sensitive information, or matters where the agency may face litigation. Legal advisors can add rigour to the analysis but can also add time to the process, and their involvement sometimes leads to more conservative withholding decisions than might otherwise occur.

Senior officials are involved when requests are politically sensitive, high-profile, or likely to attract media attention. In departments, the chief executive or a deputy chief executive will often sign off on the most significant responses. The involvement of senior officials can improve the quality of the decision (because they bring broader perspective and greater authority) but can also create bottlenecks, because their time is in high demand.

The Minister's office may be involved through the consultation or notification mechanisms described earlier in this chapter. The Minister's office typically includes political advisors and private secretaries who manage the flow of OIA-related information to and from the Minister. Their involvement can add a political dimension to the processing of a request, which may or may not be visible to you as the requester.

For you as a requester, the practical takeaway is this: your request is not being considered by a single person sitting at a desk reading your letter. It is being processed through a system that involves multiple people, multiple stages, and multiple forms of review. This system is designed to produce accurate and defensible decisions, but it is also complex and, at times, slow. Understanding the system helps you engage with it more effectively, set realistic expectations about timeframes, and identify where things may have gone wrong if the process breaks down.

CHAPTER 8

Time Limits, Extensions, and Transfers

The OIA imposes time limits on agencies for a reason: without them, requests could languish indefinitely. Understanding how these time limits work, what can extend or reset them, and what your options are when they are not met, is essential to holding agencies accountable and ensuring you receive a timely response.

The 20 Working Day Maximum

The central time limit in the OIA is straightforward. An agency must make and communicate a decision on your request "as soon as reasonably practicable" and no later than 20 working days after the day the request is received.

There are two separate obligations packed into that sentence, and the distinction matters. The first is the "as soon as reasonably practicable" standard. This means that the agency should not treat 20 working days as a target, but as an outer limit. If the request is simple and the information is readily available, the agency should respond well before day 20. The second is the hard backstop of 20 working days. Once this deadline has passed (unless a valid extension has been made), the agency is in breach of its statutory obligations, and the failure to respond is deemed to be a refusal of your request, which you can complain about to the Ombudsman.

In practice, as many requesters and commentators have observed, the "as soon as reasonably practicable" standard tends to be overshadowed by the 20-day backstop. For simple requests, agencies generally respond well within the limit. For anything of moderate complexity or political sensitivity, the 20-day deadline becomes the effective target. And for some requests, even that deadline is missed.

When the clock starts

The 20 working day count starts on the first working day after the day the request is received by the agency. If your request is received on a Tuesday, day 1 is Wednesday. If it is received on a Friday afternoon, day 1 is Monday. If your request is received outside business hours (for example, by email at 10pm on a Wednesday), it is still treated as received on that day, and the count starts the next working day. There is no requirement for the date of receipt to fall on a working day or within business hours.

What counts as a "working day"

A "working day" is any day of the week other than Saturday, Sunday, national public holidays, and the Christmas/New Year closedown period.
Under the OIA, the closedown period runs from 25 December to 15 January inclusive. Under LGOIMA, it runs from 20 December to 10 January inclusive. These days are not working days and do not count toward the 20-day limit. LGOIMA also excludes regional anniversary days for the relevant region.

The national public holidays that are excluded are: Waitangi Day, Good Friday, Easter Monday, Anzac Day, the King's Birthday, Matariki, and Labour Day.

The Office of the Ombudsman provides an online calculator on its website (www.ombudsman.parliament.nz) that will calculate the 20 working day deadline for you based on the date of receipt. This is a useful tool for tracking your requests.

What the agency must communicate

The agency's decision, communicated within the 20 working day deadline, must state whether the request is granted, and if so, in what manner the information will be made available and whether a charge will be imposed. If the request is refused in whole or in part, the agency must give the reason for the refusal and advise you of your right to complain to the Ombudsman.

When the Clock Resets

If you amend or clarify your request after submitting it, the amended or clarified version will generally be treated as a new request, and the 20 working day clock will restart from the day after the new version is received.

There is, however, an important exception. If the agency was the one that asked you to amend or clarify the request, and it did not do so within seven working days of receiving your original request, the clock does not reset. The original 20 working day deadline continues to apply.

This rule creates an incentive for agencies to identify problems with the scope of a request early. If the agency contacts you within the first seven working days to seek clarification, and you provide a clarified request, the clock restarts. If the agency waits until day 15 to raise a problem, it cannot restart the clock and must still meet the original deadline.

From your perspective, the practical implications are twofold. First, respond promptly to any request for clarification from the agency, because any delay on your part delays the restart of the clock and therefore the eventual response. Second, be aware that if you volunteer a clarification or amendment of your own initiative (rather than in response to a request from the agency), this will always restart the clock, regardless of timing.

Extensions

The agency can extend the 20 working day time limit, but only on specific grounds, for a reasonable period, and subject to procedural requirements.

The two grounds for extension

Section 15A of the OIA (section 14 of the LGOIMA) permits an extension in two circumstances:

Volume or complexity of information. The agency can extend if the request is for a large quantity of official information, or if meeting the request requires searching through a large quantity of information, and meeting the original time limit would unreasonably interfere with the agency's operations.

Consultations required. The agency can extend if consultations necessary to make a proper decision on the request cannot reasonably be completed within the original time limit. This covers both consultation with third parties (whose interests might be affected by release) and consultation with Ministers or other agencies.

These are the only two grounds. An agency cannot extend simply because it is busy, because the request is politically sensitive, because staff are on leave, or because the information has not yet been located. The ground relied on must genuinely exist.

What a valid extension notice must contain

The notice of extension must be given to you within 20 working days of the agency receiving your request. It must contain four things:

1. The period of the extension (that is, the new deadline).
2. The reasons for the extension.
3. A statement that you have the right to complain to the Ombudsman about the extension.
4. Such other information as is necessary.

An extension notice that does not specify the period, or does not give reasons, or is sent after the 20 working day period has expired, is not a valid extension.

The requirement that extensions be for a "reasonable period"

The legislation says that an extension must be for "a reasonable period of time having regard to the circumstances." This is deliberately open-ended. What is reasonable will depend on the nature and volume of the information, the complexity of the withholding decisions, and the extent of consultation required. An extension of a few additional working days for a straightforward consultation might be reasonable. An extension of several months, with no explanation of why so long is needed, would not be.

If you think the period of an extension is unreasonable, you can complain to the Ombudsman, who has the power to review the extension decision.

The rule that extensions cannot be made after the original 20 working days have passed

This is one of the most important and frequently misunderstood rules in the OIA. The extension must be effected by giving notice to you within 20 working days of the request being received. Once those 20 working days have passed, the power to extend is spent. The agency cannot retrospectively extend the deadline after it has already missed it.

The legislation also permits only a single extension on any given request. Once an extension has been made, the agency cannot make a further extension for the same request. The extension must be set at a level that the agency genuinely believes will be sufficient, because there is no second chance.

In practice, this means that agencies must make their extension decision early in the process. An agency that waits until day 19 to realise it will not meet the deadline, and then rushes out a last-minute extension notice, is technically compliant but is not acting in the spirit of the legislation. Conversely, an agency that misses the 20-day window entirely has no power to extend and is deemed to have refused the request.

Transfers to Another Agency

If the information you have requested is not held by the agency you sent your request to, or if it is more closely connected with the functions of another agency, the receiving agency must transfer the request (or the relevant part of it) to the other agency.

The 10 working day deadline for transfers

The decision to transfer must be made promptly and no later than 10 working days after the agency received your request (unless an extension of this deadline has been made under section 15A). The agency must inform you of the transfer.

The 10-day deadline for transfers is shorter than the 20-day deadline for decisions, because transfers are supposed to happen at the beginning of the process, not at the end. The purpose is to get the request to the right agency as quickly as possible, so that the substantive work of finding and reviewing the information can begin without unnecessary delay.

In practice, however, the 10-day transfer deadline is sometimes breached. Research into the operation of the OIA has found that the transfer decision is often made late in the process, particularly when the transfer involves shifting responsibility from a department to a Minister, and the question of who should make the decision only becomes apparent after the information has been identified and the withholding issues have been considered. This late transfer problem is a recognised weakness in the system.

The clock restarting after a transfer

When a request is transferred to another agency, the 20 working day clock restarts from the day after the transfer is received by the new agency. This means that a transfer effectively gives the system an additional 20 working days (on top of however many days elapsed before the transfer was made). From your perspective, a transfer always means delay.

What should be transferred along with the request

When an agency transfers your request to another agency, it should transfer not just the request itself but also any relevant information it holds. The Ombudsman has made clear that agencies should identify all relevant information they hold and send it to the receiving agency along with the request. This is particularly important when a request is transferred from a department to a Minister, because the department may hold information that the Minister does not, and transferring the information along with the request avoids the requester losing access to material that the department could have released.

The agency should also explain to you, when notifying you of the transfer, why the transfer is being made and that all relevant information held by the transferring agency has been sent along with the request.

Transfers to Ministers and the complications that arise

Transfers between departments and Ministers are among the most contentious aspects of OIA practice. As discussed in Chapter 2, a transfer shifts decision-making responsibility from the department to the Minister, and some requesters view this with suspicion, perceiving it as a tactic to delay or to shift the decision to someone more likely to withhold.

The Ombudsman has emphasised that transfers must be based on genuine statutory grounds. A department cannot transfer simply because the Minister wants to control the response, or because there is a disagreement between the department and the Minister about whether information should be released. The test is whether the information is not held by the department (straightforward cases where the Minister holds it and the department does not), or whether it is more closely connected with the functions of the Minister.

If you are suspicious that a transfer to a Minister has been made for improper reasons, you can complain to the Ombudsman. Although the OIA does not expressly give the Ombudsman jurisdiction to review transfer decisions, the Ombudsman can investigate complaints about transfers under the Ombudsmen Act 1975, provided the agency that made the transfer is subject to that Act.

The "Undue Delay" Obligation

The time limits discussed above relate to the decision on your request. But there is a separate obligation that applies to the release of information after the decision has been made. Section 28(5) of the OIA provides that "undue delay" in making official information available is deemed to be a refusal of the request, which can be investigated by the Ombudsman.

This means that even after the agency has decided to release information, it must do so promptly. It cannot sit on the decision and release the information weeks or months later. In some cases, a brief delay after the decision may be justified if the agency needs time to prepare the information for release (for example, by scanning documents, applying redactions, or compiling electronic files). But the delay must not be "undue."

The Ombudsman has upheld complaints where agencies delayed release by even a single day for improper reasons. In one case, a Minister delayed couriering information to a requester by one day so that the requester would receive it at the same time as a newspaper to which the information had also been provided. The Chief Ombudsman found the delay was "undue," noting that any acceptance that the OIA permitted such delays would inevitably lead to longer ones.

What to Do When an Agency Is Running Late

Despite the clear statutory time limits, late responses are a persistent problem. Here is what you can do when an agency is running late.

Follow up with the agency. If the 20 working day deadline has passed (or is about to pass) without a response, contact the agency and ask for an explanation. Sometimes a simple reminder is enough to prompt action. Ask when you can expect to receive a response, and make a note of the answer.

Check whether a valid extension was made. If the agency claims to have extended the deadline, check whether the extension notice was sent within 20 working days of receipt of your request, whether it specified the period of extension and the reasons for it, and whether it advised you of your right to complain to the Ombudsman. If any of these requirements were not met, the extension may not be valid.

Complain to the Ombudsman. If the statutory deadline has passed without a response and without a valid extension, the agency's failure to respond is deemed to be a refusal of your request. You can complain to the

Ombudsman, who has the power to investigate delays and to recommend that the agency respond. You can make your complaint in writing (including by email) to info@ombudsman.parliament.nz.

Complain about undue delay within the time limit. Even if the 20 working days have not yet expired, you may be able to complain if the agency is taking longer than is reasonably necessary. The obligation to respond "as soon as reasonably practicable" applies throughout the 20-day period. If the agency is clearly dragging its feet on a simple request that could have been answered in a few days, a complaint about undue delay may be appropriate.

Note the deemed refusal. Under section 28(4) of the OIA, a failure to respond within the statutory time limit (or any extended time limit) is deemed to be a refusal. Under section 28(5), undue delay in making information available is also deemed to be a refusal. Both of these deemed refusals trigger your right to complain to the Ombudsman. You do not need to wait for the agency to formally refuse your request before you can complain. The failure to respond in time is itself the refusal.

There is no penalty for agencies that breach the time limits. Unlike some overseas jurisdictions, New Zealand has no system of fines or sanctions for non-compliance with OIA deadlines. The Ombudsman can investigate, form opinions, and make recommendations, but cannot impose penalties. This is one of the most commonly criticised aspects of the system. The lack of effective sanctions means that, for some agencies, there is little practical consequence for habitual lateness. For requesters, the Ombudsman's investigation process, while free and accessible, is itself slow, and the result is a recommendation, not an order. Nevertheless, complaining to the Ombudsman remains the most effective remedy available, and agencies generally take Ombudsman recommendations seriously.

PART FOUR

UNDERSTANDING REFUSAL

CHAPTER 10

The Framework for Withholding

This chapter is the gateway to Part Four of this book, which deals with refusals. Before we examine the individual withholding grounds in detail (Chapters 11 to 13), it is important to understand the overall framework within which those grounds operate. The framework has a clear logic, and understanding that logic will help you assess whether a refusal is justified, identify where an agency may have gone wrong, and frame an effective complaint if you need to make one.

The Starting Point Is Always the Principle of Availability

Every consideration of whether to withhold official information must begin from the same place: the principle of availability, set out in section 5 of the OIA (and in identical terms in section 5 of LGOIMA). The principle states that information shall be made available unless there is good reason for withholding it.

This is not a platitude. It is the foundational rule of the entire system. It means that the default position for every request is release. The burden falls on the agency to identify a specific reason for withholding, not on you to justify why you should receive the information. If the agency cannot point to a good reason, the information must be released.

The Ombudsmen have consistently stressed that the Act must receive a fair, large, and liberal interpretation, consistent with its purposes of increasing the availability of official information, enabling public participation, and promoting accountability. The withholding grounds are "tightly drawn" and must be read in the context of this overarching commitment to openness.

The principle of availability does not mean that everything must be released. The OIA recognises that there are legitimate reasons for withholding some information. But it does mean that withholding is the exception, not the rule, and that any exception must be justified on the specific grounds provided by the legislation.

The Three Categories of Refusal Grounds

The OIA provides an exhaustive list of reasons on which a request may be refused. There are no other grounds. An agency cannot manufacture new reasons for withholding by relying on the purposes of the Act (such as the reference to protecting official information in section 4(c)), or by invoking general principles like the "public interest" in secrecy. The withholding grounds set the outer limits of what can be refused.

These grounds fall into three distinct categories, each with its own characteristics and legal tests. Understanding the differences between these categories is essential.

Conclusive reasons (section 6)

The strongest grounds for withholding are found in section 6 of the OIA (and section 6 of LGOIMA). These are called "conclusive" reasons because, if they apply, the information can be withheld without further inquiry. There is no public interest override. If an agency establishes that releasing the information would be likely to cause one of the harms identified in section 6, that is the end of the matter.

The conclusive grounds protect the most sensitive interests: the security and defence of New Zealand, its international relations, the entrusting of information in confidence by other governments or international organisations, the maintenance of the law (including fair trial rights), personal safety, and (under the OIA only) the economy of New Zealand from serious damage through premature disclosure of certain economic or financial policy decisions.

The legal test for section 6 is that disclosure "would be likely" to cause the prejudice in question. The Court of Appeal has interpreted this phrase to mean a "serious or real and substantial risk" to the protected interest, a risk that "might well eventuate." This is a lower threshold than the test for section 9 grounds, but it still requires more than mere possibility. The agency must be able to identify, with sufficient particularity, the nature of the prejudicial effect and explain how it would occur.

The conclusive grounds are discussed in detail in Chapter 11.

Good reasons subject to the public interest test (section 9)

The most commonly invoked withholding grounds are found in section 9 of the OIA (section 7 of LGOIMA). These are called "good reasons," and they differ from the conclusive grounds in two critical respects.

First, the legal test is higher. Section 9 applies "if, and only if, the withholding of the information is necessary" to avoid prejudice to one of the identified interests. "Necessary" has been interpreted to mean "reasonably necessary." This is a more demanding standard than the "would be likely" test in section 6.

Second, and most importantly, the section 9 grounds are subject to a public interest test. Even if a ground for withholding is established, the information must still be released if, in the circumstances of the particular case, the public interest in disclosure outweighs the need to withhold. This public interest override is one of the most powerful features of the New Zealand legislation. It means that the analysis does not stop once a withholding ground is made out. The agency must go on to consider whether the balance of the public interest nevertheless favours release.

The section 9 grounds protect a wide range of interests: privacy, commercial position, trade secrets, confidential information, the free and frank expression of opinions, legal professional privilege, negotiations, constitutional conventions, confidential advice to government, and others. These are the grounds you will encounter most frequently in practice, and they are discussed in detail in Chapter 12.

Administrative reasons (section 18)

The third category comprises the administrative or procedural grounds for refusal, found in section 18 of the OIA (section 17 of LGOIMA). These are not about protecting substantive interests. They deal with practical limitations on the ability of agencies to respond to requests.

The administrative grounds include: that the information is not held and cannot be found (section 18(e)); that the information cannot be made available without substantial collation or research (section 18(f)); that the information is or will soon be publicly available (section 18(d)); that release would be contrary to an enactment or would constitute contempt of court or the House (section 18(c)); and that the request is frivolous, vexatious, or trivial (section 18(h)).

Administrative grounds are not subject to a public interest test. If they apply, there is no need to weigh the public interest in release against the reason for withholding. However, reliance on the administrative grounds is discretionary, not mandatory. An agency may choose to release information even if an administrative ground for refusal exists, particularly where there is a clear and compelling public interest in making the information available.

The administrative grounds are discussed in detail in Chapter 13.

Partial Release

One of the most important features of the OIA is the concept of partial release, provided for in section 17. Where a document contains some information that there is good reason to withhold and some information that can be released, the agency is not entitled to refuse the entire document. Instead, it must release the document with the withheld information deleted or altered.

In practice, this means redaction: blacking out or removing the specific passages, sentences, names, figures, or paragraphs that are subject to a withholding ground, while releasing everything else. You will frequently receive documents with sections redacted, and each redaction should correspond to a specific withholding ground.

Section 17 is not mandatory in the sense that there is no absolute obligation to make redactions in every case. The Danks Committee recognised that redaction may be impractical where the information to be withheld forms so integral or large a part of the document that the remainder would be meaningless or misleading. But the principle of availability means that an agency should consider partial release before refusing a request outright. The Ombudsmen have used the duty of reasonable assistance to requesters (section 13) to support the conclusion that agencies must consider whether partial release is possible.

When an agency makes a document available with deletions, it must give you the reason for withholding the deleted information, and must give you the grounds in support of that reason if you ask. This obligation is subject to section 10 (the "neither confirm nor deny" provision, discussed below).

From your perspective as a requester, partial release is important because it means that a refusal is rarely all-or-nothing. Even where some information is legitimately withheld, you should receive everything else. If you receive a response that appears to withhold entire documents rather than redacting specific passages, consider whether the agency has properly considered its obligation under section 17. If you believe it has not, this is a ground for complaint to the Ombudsman.

Decision-makers should also be warned that improper redactions are subject to review. In one well-known incident, a Minister released a report with unjustifiable deletions to a requester who already had an unredacted copy. Improper deletions are, of course, subject to investigation by the Ombudsman.

The "Neither Confirm nor Deny" Power (Section 10)

Section 10 of the OIA (section 8 of LGOIMA) gives agencies a power that is more far-reaching than ordinary withholding. It allows an agency to refuse to confirm or deny the existence or non-existence of the information you have requested.

This is sometimes called the "NCND" response. Instead of telling you that the information exists but is being withheld, the agency says, in effect, "we are not prepared to tell you whether or not we hold information of the kind you have described."

The power exists because, in some cases, the very act of confirming that information exists (or does not exist) would itself cause harm to a protected interest. To use a classic example: if you ask a law enforcement agency whether it holds surveillance files on a particular individual, and the agency responds by withholding the files, you know that the files exist. The confirmation of their existence may itself prejudice the maintenance of the law. Section 10 allows the agency to avoid this problem by declining to say whether the information exists at all.

Section 10 can be invoked where confirming or denying the existence of the information would be likely to prejudice any of the interests protected by sections 6, 7, or 9(2)(b) of the OIA. It was envisaged by the Danks Committee as a power to be used rarely, in areas such as plans to deal with terrorists, police sources, and certain highly delicate international negotiations.

The practical impact of a section 10 response is that you receive very little information. The agency will not tell you whether it holds the information, will not tell you the specific withholding ground it would rely on (because doing so might itself confirm or deny something), and may give only a generic explanation of why the section 10 response has been issued.

Section 10 responses can be reviewed by the Ombudsman. If you receive a section 10 response and believe it has been used inappropriately, you can complain. The Ombudsman will have access to the information (if it exists) and can form an independent view on whether the section 10 response was justified.

In the reported Ombudsman case law, section 10 has been upheld most commonly in the context of national security and intelligence. In one case, a requester sought information about intelligence conferences. The Director of the Security Intelligence Service issued a section 10 notice, and the Ombudsman accepted that the Director's reliance on section 10 was reasonable and proper, given the low threshold for prejudice under section 6 and the absence of a public interest balancing test for that section.

Section 10 also governs the giving of reasons for other types of decisions. Where a refusal, a deletion, or a decision to provide information in a non-preferred format would require the agency to confirm or deny the existence of information in a way that would prejudice a protected interest, section 10 allows the agency to withhold that explanation as well.

The Requirement to Give Reasons for Any Refusal

The OIA does not allow agencies to refuse requests silently. When a request is refused, or when information is deleted from a document, or when information is provided in a manner other than that preferred by the requester, the agency must give you the reason for its decision.

This obligation operates at two levels.

The first level is the reason itself. The agency must tell you which statutory provision it is relying on. For example, it might say that information has been withheld under section 9(2)(g)(i) to protect free and frank opinions, or under section 6(d) to protect personal safety, or under section 18(f) because the information cannot be made available without substantial collation or research. The statutory reason must be provided at the time the decision is communicated to you.

The second level is the grounds in support of that reason. If you ask (and you should always ask if the reason alone does not adequately explain the decision), the agency must give you the grounds that support its reliance on the stated reason. This means it must explain, with some specificity, why it considers the withholding ground to be made out. For a section 9 refusal, this should include the agency's assessment of the harm that would result from disclosure and its application of the public interest test. For a section 6 refusal, it should include an explanation of how disclosure would be likely to cause the relevant prejudice.

There is one exception. The agency does not have to give the grounds if doing so would itself prejudice the interests protected by sections 6, 7, or 9 (and, in the case of section 9, there is no countervailing public interest in giving the grounds). This exception is narrow and applies mainly in the context of section 10 responses, where the agency cannot explain its reasoning without revealing the very thing it is trying to protect.

From your perspective, the requirement to give reasons is one of your most important tools. A refusal that simply cites a section number without any explanation of why that section applies is inadequate. If you receive such a response, write back and ask for the grounds in support of the reason. The agency is legally obligated to provide them. The grounds it gives will help you assess whether the refusal is justified, and they will form the basis of any complaint to the Ombudsman.

The requirement to give reasons also imposes a discipline on agencies. It forces them to articulate their reasoning, to identify the specific harm they are trying to prevent, and to demonstrate that they have genuinely engaged with the statutory tests rather than simply invoking a withholding ground reflexively. Agencies that cannot adequately explain the grounds for their decision are, in the Ombudsman's experience, more likely to have applied the withholding grounds incorrectly.

Always ask for the grounds. It costs you nothing, and it produces information that is essential for any challenge to the refusal.

CHAPTER 11

Conclusive Reasons for Withholding (Section 6)

The conclusive withholding grounds in section 6 of the OIA (and section 6 of LGOIMA) represent the outer boundary of government secrecy under the official information legislation. They protect the interests that Parliament has judged to be so important that, if disclosure would be likely to cause harm to them, no further analysis is required. This chapter explains what makes these grounds different from all the others, sets out the legal test, examines each ground in turn, and offers practical guidance on what to look for when an agency invokes section 6 in response to your request.

What Makes Section 6 Grounds "Conclusive"

The withholding grounds in section 6 are called "conclusive" for a single, critical reason: they are not subject to the public interest test that applies to the section 9 grounds. If an agency establishes that disclosure of the requested information would be likely to cause one of the specific harms identified in section 6, the information can be withheld. There is no further step of weighing the public interest in release against the need to protect the information. The analysis stops once the ground is made out.

This is a significant departure from the general approach of the OIA, which is built on the idea that competing interests must be balanced. The Danks Committee, which designed the legislation, was deliberate about this. It considered that in the areas covered by section 6, the interests at stake were so fundamental that protection from disclosure should be absolute if disclosure was likely to prejudice them. As the Committee put it in its General Report, these considerations led it to propose that in these areas, "protection from disclosure shall be absolute if disclosure is likely to prejudice essential interests including the continued flow of information."

Some commentators have criticised this approach. Two requesters interviewed in the Arie research thought it was anomalous for there to be no capacity to consider the public interest in relation to section 6 matters, and suggested that it was time to update the Act by bringing all the withholding grounds into a single and consistent framework. The Law Commission's 2012 review did not recommend this change, and section 6 remains as the Danks Committee designed it.

The practical consequence for you as a requester is that section 6 refusals are harder to challenge than section 9 refusals. You cannot argue that the public interest in release outweighs the need to withhold, because the legislation does not permit that argument. Your challenge must instead focus on whether the ground is actually made out: whether the predicted harm is real, whether it is sufficiently particularised, and whether disclosure would genuinely be "likely" to cause it.

The "Would Be Likely" Threshold

Section 6 applies where the making available of the information "would be likely" to cause one of the specified harms. This phrase has been interpreted by the Court of Appeal in the leading case of *Commissioner of Police v Ombudsman* (1988).

The Court held that "would be likely" means "a serious or real and substantial risk to a protected interest, a risk that might well eventuate." This is more than mere possibility. An agency cannot invoke section 6 on the basis of a theoretical or speculative risk that harm might occur. There must be a genuine, identifiable risk that is grounded in the specific circumstances of the case.

At the same time, the threshold is lower than the test for section 9, where the withholding must be "necessary" to avoid prejudice to the protected interest. "Necessary" (interpreted as "reasonably necessary") requires a closer connection between disclosure and harm than "would be likely." This difference in thresholds reflects the greater weight Parliament has placed on the interests protected by section 6.

In assessing whether the threshold is met, both the content of the information and the context in which it was generated are relevant. The

Ombudsman's guidance identifies four factors that should be considered in most cases, regardless of which subsection is relied on:

Who generated or supplied the information at issue? Information from a foreign intelligence service, for example, carries a different weight from information generated internally by a New Zealand department.

What does the information reveal? The sensitivity of the content itself is obviously relevant. Information about the deployment of military personnel in an active operation carries a different risk from historical information about a long-concluded exercise.

In what context was the information generated or supplied? Information provided in confidence as part of a diplomatic exchange, for example, may attract section 6 protection that would not apply to the same information if it were publicly known from another source.

Timing. Where the information relates to a particular process, what stage had been reached at the time the request was received and what will happen next? The risk of harm from disclosure may be high while a process is ongoing and negligible once it has concluded.

The agency must be able to identify, with sufficient particularity, the nature of the prejudicial effect and explain how such prejudice will occur. A bare assertion that disclosure would be prejudicial is not enough. The Ombudsman will expect to see a reasoned explanation of the specific harm that is anticipated.

The Specific Grounds

Section 6(a): Security, Defence, and International Relations

Section 6(a) of the OIA provides that information can be withheld if its disclosure would be likely to prejudice the security or defence of New Zealand or the international relations of the Government of New Zealand.

This is the broadest of the conclusive grounds and covers three overlapping areas.

Security refers to the safety and stability of the state, including protection against threats such as espionage, terrorism, and sabotage. It extends to the activities of the intelligence and security agencies (the NZSIS and the GCSB), as well as to information held by other agencies that relates to national security.

Defence covers information relating to the military defence of New Zealand, including military operations, deployments, capabilities, and plans.

International relations covers information whose disclosure would be likely to prejudice the Government's conduct of its relationships with other countries and international organisations. This is a broad category that can encompass diplomatic correspondence, negotiating positions, assessments of other countries' positions, and information about New Zealand's participation in international forums.

The Ombudsman has considered the application of section 6(a) in a variety of contexts, including reports on environmental damage resulting from French nuclear testing, information relating to a New Zealand candidate for the position of Director-General of the World Trade Organisation, and an application for the initiation of an anti-dumping investigation. In each case, the analysis turned on the specific content of the information and the concrete risk that disclosure would prejudice the relevant interest.

The LGOIMA equivalent is identical in wording to section 6(a) of the OIA. Prior to 2023, LGOIMA did not include a ground for security and defence, but was amended to align with the OIA.

Section 6(b): Entrusting of Information in Confidence

Section 6(b) provides that information can be withheld if its disclosure would be likely to prejudice the entrusting of information to the Government of New Zealand on a basis of confidence by the government of any other country or any agency of such a government, or by any international organisation.

This ground recognises a simple reality of international relations: governments share sensitive information with each other, and they do so on the understanding that the receiving government will protect the confidentiality of that information. If New Zealand were to disclose information entrusted to it in confidence by another government, the flow of such information might diminish, to New Zealand's detriment.

The key elements are that the information must have been entrusted to the New Zealand Government (not merely transmitted in the ordinary course of business), that it must have been entrusted on a basis of confidence, and that disclosure must be likely to prejudice the willingness of other governments or international organisations to continue providing information on that basis.

The Ombudsman has considered this ground in cases involving papers presented to the New Zealand Government leading to a decision to withdraw troops from Bosnia, and information relating to a proposed visit to New Zealand by a United States naval vessel.

Section 6(c): Maintenance of the Law

Section 6(c) provides that information can be withheld if its disclosure would be likely to prejudice the maintenance of the law, including the prevention, investigation, and detection of offences, and the right to a fair trial.

This is one of the most commonly encountered section 6 grounds, because it covers a wide range of law enforcement and judicial interests.

The reference to the "prevention, investigation, and detection of offences" protects police operational methods, intelligence-gathering techniques, the identity of informants and undercover officers, details of ongoing investigations, and other information whose disclosure could compromise law enforcement activities.

The reference to the "right to a fair trial" protects information whose disclosure could prejudice the ability of a person to receive a fair hearing in criminal or civil proceedings. This might include witness statements, prosecution strategies, evidence not yet disclosed to the defence, or information subject to suppression orders.

The Ombudsman has considered this ground in cases involving information about the alleged sexual violation of a hospital patient by a staff member (where information was withheld pending the outcome of proceedings to protect fair trial rights), police details of the diversion of a taxi licence applicant, and details of APEC security arrangements.

Section 6(d): Endangering the Safety of Any Person

Section 6(d) provides that information can be withheld if its disclosure would be likely to endanger the safety of any person.

This is the most personal of the conclusive grounds. It is designed to protect individuals from physical harm that might result from the disclosure of official information. It has been applied in cases where disclosure could expose a person to violence, harassment, or intimidation.

The Ombudsman has considered this ground in a case involving a child's prize-giving results, where the child had requested that the results not be provided to a non-custodial parent because of the use made by that parent of other information. The Ombudsman accepted that section 6(d) applied in those circumstances.

Section 6(d) does not require proof that harm will certainly occur. Consistent with the general "would be likely" threshold, there must be a serious and real risk to a person's safety, but certainty is not required. The agency does not need to wait until actual threats have been made or acted upon. However, there must be more than a remote or speculative possibility of danger.

As with the other conclusive grounds, section 6(d) is not subject to the public interest test. If there is a real and substantial risk to a person's safety, the information can be withheld regardless of any countervailing public interest in disclosure.

Section 6(e): Serious Damage to the Economy of New Zealand (OIA Only)

Section 6(e) provides that information can be withheld if its disclosure would be likely to damage seriously the economy of New Zealand by disclosing prematurely decisions to change or continue Government economic or financial policies relating to exchange rates, overseas exchange transactions, the regulation of banking or credit, taxation, prices and costs, wages and incomes, government borrowing, or overseas trade agreements.

This ground exists only in the OIA. There is no equivalent in LGOIMA, because local government agencies do not make the kinds of national economic and financial policy decisions that section 6(e) is designed to protect.

The key word in section 6(e) is "prematurely." The ground does not protect economic policy decisions from disclosure forever. It protects them from premature disclosure, that is, disclosure before the Government has announced its decision or the decision has taken effect. Once the decision is public, section 6(e) no longer applies to the information about that decision (though other withholding grounds might).

The Ombudsman has considered this ground in a case involving information about producer board reforms.

How These Grounds Are Applied in Practice

The Ombudsman's published case notes provide the most detailed publicly available guidance on how the section 6 grounds are applied. Several themes emerge from the case law.

Specificity is required. The agency must be able to explain precisely how disclosure would prejudice the protected interest. A generic claim that "releasing this information would harm national security" or "could prejudice law enforcement" is not sufficient. The Ombudsman will want to see a detailed account of the nature of the information, the specific harm that would result from disclosure, and the connection between the two.

Context matters. Information that might need to be withheld under section 6 in one context may not need to be withheld in another. Historical information about a concluded military operation, for example, may no longer pose a risk to security or defence, even though the same information would have attracted section 6 protection while the operation was ongoing. The passage of time, the conclusion of a process, or the publication of the information from another source can all affect whether the ground is made out.

The Ombudsman conducts a genuine review. Although the Ombudsman may give considerable weight to the views of agencies on matters within their expertise (particularly on security and intelligence matters), the review is not a rubber stamp. The Ombudsman examines the withheld information, considers the agency's reasons, and forms an independent view. In some cases, the Ombudsman has disagreed with the agency's assessment and recommended release.

Partial release should be considered. Even where section 6 applies to some of the information in a document, other information in the same document may not be covered. The agency should consider whether partial release under section 17 is possible, providing the document with the protected information redacted.

What to Look for When an Agency Invokes Section 6

If you receive a refusal based on section 6, here are the questions you should ask yourself before deciding whether to accept the refusal or complain to the Ombudsman.

Has the agency identified the specific subsection? A refusal that simply cites "section 6" without specifying which paragraph (a) through (e) is inadequate. Each subsection protects a different interest, and the agency must be clear about which interest is at stake.

Has the agency explained the harm? The agency must be able to explain how disclosure would prejudice the protected interest. If the refusal letter says nothing more than "release would be likely to prejudice national security," ask for the grounds in support of that reason. The agency is required to provide them, unless doing so would itself prejudice the protected interest (in which case it may issue a section 10 response).

Is the predicted harm real and substantial? The "would be likely" threshold requires more than mere possibility. Consider whether the harm the agency is describing is genuine, grounded in the specific circumstances, and of a kind that might well eventuate. If the predicted harm seems remote, speculative, or theoretical, there may be grounds for a complaint.

Has the context changed? Section 6 applies at the time the request is made. If the information relates to a process that has since concluded, a risk that has since passed, or a matter that has since been made public through other channels, the basis for withholding may no longer exist. Consider whether the circumstances have changed in a way that undermines the agency's reliance on section 6.

Has the agency considered partial release? If only part of the information is protected by section 6, the rest should be released with appropriate redactions. If the agency has withheld an entire document and you suspect that only portions of it are truly sensitive, this is a ground for complaint.

Is section 6 the right ground? Sometimes agencies invoke section 6 when section 9 would be more appropriate, because section 6 avoids the need to engage with the public interest test. If the harm the agency is describing seems more like the kind of interest protected by section 9 (for example, privacy, commercial sensitivity, or free and frank opinions) than the kind protected by section 6 (security, defence, law enforcement, personal safety), the agency may be relying on the wrong provision. The choice of provision matters, because section 9 would require the agency to consider the public interest in release, while section 6 does not.

If you are unsure whether a section 6 refusal is justified, a complaint to the Ombudsman costs nothing and puts the matter before an independent reviewer who has full access to the withheld information and the expertise to assess whether the ground is properly made out.

CHAPTER 12

Good Reasons for Withholding (Section 9)

Section 9 is where the overwhelming majority of OIA disputes play out. It is the provision you will encounter most often in agency responses, the provision most frequently challenged through the Ombudsman, and the provision that gives rise to the most difficult questions about the balance between openness and protection. This chapter explains how section 9 works and gives you a practical guide to the most commonly invoked grounds, written from the requester's perspective.

How Section 9 Works

Section 9 is structured as a two-step test. First, the agency must show that withholding is "necessary" to protect one of the interests specified in section 9(2). Second, even if withholding is necessary to protect that interest, the agency must consider whether the public interest in release outweighs the need to withhold.

The word "necessary" sets a high bar. It means more than "desirable" or "convenient" or "preferred by the agency." The agency must demonstrate that there is a specific, identifiable harm that would result from disclosure, and that withholding is required to prevent that harm. A vague assertion that release might cause some unspecified difficulty is not sufficient. The Ombudsman expects agencies to articulate, with reference to the specific information at issue, what the harm would be, why it would occur, and why it cannot be managed in any other way (for example, through partial release, release with contextual explanation, or release at a later date).

This two-step structure means that even when a withholding ground is technically made out, the information may still need to be released if the public interest demands it. The public interest test is not an afterthought or a formality. It is an integral part of the analysis, and the Ombudsman expects agencies to engage with it genuinely in every case where a section 9 ground is invoked.

The Public Interest Test

Section 9(1) provides that a good reason for withholding exists "unless, in the circumstances of the particular case, the withholding of that information is outweighed by other considerations which render it desirable, in the public interest, to make that information available."

The public interest test requires a balancing exercise. On one side of the scales are the reasons for withholding (the specific harm that disclosure would cause to the protected interest). On the other side are the reasons for release (the public interest considerations that favour making the information available). The test is applied to the particular information in the particular circumstances of the case, not in the abstract. Both the strength of the harm from release and the strength of the public interest in disclosure will vary from case to case.

The Ombudsman's detailed guide to the public interest test identifies the following categories of consideration that may favour release, though the Ombudsman emphasises that the categories of public interest are not closed and will depend entirely on the circumstances.

Transparency: there is a general public interest in the transparent conduct of public affairs. Transparency enhances public trust, maintains integrity, and discourages corruption and bad practices.

Participation: the OIA explicitly recognises that public participation in decision-making enhances respect for the law and promotes good government. There is a public interest in disclosing information that enables people to understand and debate issues, and to participate in decision-making processes that affect them. Timely access to information can be critical here, because there is often a deadline after which the information loses its value for participation purposes.

Accountability: there is a public interest in promoting the accountability of Ministers, agencies, and public servants for how they make decisions, perform their functions, spend public money, and respond when things go wrong. Accountability considerations are usually strongest after a decision has been made, because the public is then entitled to understand and scrutinise the process that led to it.

Administration of justice: there is a public interest in enabling people to pursue their legal rights and remedies, and in ensuring procedural fairness. If a requester needs the information to respond to allegations against them, to pursue a legal claim, or to participate effectively in a legal or administrative process, this weighs in favour of release.

Health, safety, and the environment: there is a public interest in keeping the public informed about risks and dangers to public health, safety, or the environment, and about the measures being taken to address them.

The Ombudsman's guidance also identifies several factors that can affect the weight of the public interest in disclosure. The significance of the subject matter is relevant: the more important the issue, the stronger the public interest in disclosure. The level of public interest, debate, or controversy about the topic is relevant: if the subject has generated public or parliamentary concern, this may increase the weight of the public interest. However, the absence of prior public debate does not diminish the public interest, because the public may not yet be aware of the issue. The extent to which related information is already in the public domain is relevant: if some information is already known, there may be a public interest in disclosing additional information to provide a complete and accurate picture.

The public interest is not the same as "interesting to the public." Mere curiosity does not constitute a public interest in release. But nor is the public interest limited to matters of high constitutional importance. Accountability for routine government decision-making, transparency in the expenditure of public money, and the ability of affected individuals to understand why decisions were made about them are all genuine public interest considerations.

For requesters, the public interest test is your strongest argument when an agency has made out a technical case for withholding. If you believe there are public interest factors that favour release, make them explicit in your request or in any subsequent engagement with the agency. If you complain to the Ombudsman, explain the public interest factors in your complaint, and connect them specifically to the content and context of the information you are seeking.

Most Commonly Invoked Grounds

Privacy (Section 9(2)(a))

This ground protects the privacy of natural persons, including deceased natural persons. It applies only to individuals, not to corporate entities or government agencies.

The types of information commonly withheld under this ground include: names and identifying details of individuals who are mentioned in documents but are not the subject of the request; personal contact details such as home addresses, personal email addresses, and personal phone numbers; health, financial, or employment information about identifiable individuals; and information about personal relationships, family circumstances, or other private matters.

The Ombudsman assesses privacy claims by considering several factors. The nature and sensitivity of the information is important: highly sensitive personal information (such as health details, financial difficulties, or family circumstances) warrants stronger protection than routine professional information. The extent to which the information is already publicly available is relevant: if the information is already known, the privacy interest is diminished. The circumstances in which the agency obtained the information matter: if it was provided on an understanding of confidentiality, that weighs in favour of protection. Whether disclosure would be fair to the individual concerned is also considered, including whether they had any reasonable expectation about how the information would be used.

For requesters, the key limits on this ground are as follows. First, it protects only natural persons, not organisations. If an agency cites privacy to withhold information about a company, that is incorrect. Second, the privacy interest must be assessed in context. The Ombudsman has published specific guidance on the names and contact details of public sector employees, noting that in many cases there is no reasonable expectation of privacy in respect of the official actions of public servants acting in their professional capacity. The identity of the decision-maker, the author of a report, or the official who handled a particular matter will often be releasable. Third, partial release can often resolve the tension: redacting the names of individuals while releasing the substance of the information may satisfy both the privacy interest and the public interest in disclosure. Fourth, the public interest test applies. Even where privacy is genuinely engaged, release may be required if the public interest in accountability, informed debate, or the administration of justice outweighs the privacy concern.

It is worth noting that the OIA's privacy ground operates alongside, but is separate from, the Privacy Act 2020. If the Ombudsman is investigating a complaint that involves section 9(2)(a), the Ombudsman must consult with the Privacy Commissioner before forming a final opinion on whether the ground is made out.

Commercial Sensitivity (Section 9(2)(b))

This ground has two limbs. The first protects trade secrets (section 9(2)(b)(i)). The second protects information where release would be likely unreasonably to prejudice the commercial position of the person who supplied or who is the subject of the information (section 9(2)(b)(ii)).

Trade secrets are a narrow category with a high threshold. The information must be used (or capable of being used) in a trade or business, must give its owner a competitive advantage over those who do not know it, and must have been kept secret by the owner. Processes of manufacture, chemical formulae, and specialised methods of construction are classic examples. Information does not have to be technical or scientific to qualify, but the more technical the information, the more likely it will be a trade secret. There will need to be clear and convincing evidence to persuade the Ombudsman that non-technical business information (such as pricing, customer lists, or sales data) qualifies as a trade secret rather than simply commercially valuable information. The Ombudsman considers factors including the extent to which the information is known outside the business, the measures taken to guard its secrecy, its value to the owner and competitors, the effort spent developing it, and the ease with which others might duplicate it.

The commercial prejudice limb (section 9(2)(b)(ii)) is more commonly invoked and has a different structure. It protects third parties (not the agency itself) from unreasonable prejudice to their commercial position. The agency must demonstrate two things: first, that the third party has a commercial position; and second, that release of the specific information at issue would be likely to prejudice that position unreasonably. A vague reference to "commercial sensitivity" or "confidentiality" is not sufficient. The prejudice must be real, must flow from the release of the particular information, and must be unreasonable rather than merely inconvenient or uncomfortable.

The word "unreasonably" is important. Some commentators and the Ombudsman have interpreted it as incorporating an element of fairness into the assessment. Disclosure that would cause minor inconvenience may not be unreasonable. Disclosure of information that a third party was compelled to provide (for example, under a statutory reporting requirement) may involve a stronger case for unreasonableness than disclosure of information that was provided voluntarily. The public interest test also applies, so even where commercial prejudice is established, the information must be released if the public interest outweighs the commercial harm.

This ground is frequently encountered in procurement and contract contexts. Requesters often seek information about government contracts, tender processes, and the commercial arrangements between agencies and private suppliers. The Ombudsman has emphasised that the fact that information was provided in the course of a commercial relationship does not automatically make it commercially sensitive. The price paid by a government agency for goods or services involves public money and is often releasable. The terms of completed contracts, the identity of successful tenderers, and the criteria used to evaluate tenders are frequently released. Information about genuinely proprietary methods, confidential pricing structures for future bids, or details that would give a competitor an unfair advantage in a specific market is more likely to warrant protection. But even here, the agency must explain the specific prejudice, not simply assert that the information is "commercial in confidence."

Confidentiality (Section 9(2)(ba))

This ground protects information that is subject to an obligation of confidence or that any person has been or could be compelled to provide under the authority of an enactment, where release would be likely to prejudice the supply of similar information in the future (and it is in the public interest that such supply continue), or would otherwise damage the public interest.

The structure of this ground is more complex than it first appears. There are two preconditions: either the information must be subject to an obligation of confidence, or it must have been (or could have been) obtained under statutory compulsion. In either case, the agency must then show one of two consequences: either that release would be likely to prejudice the future supply of similar information (and it is in the public interest that such supply continue), or that release would otherwise damage the public interest.

The key requirement for the first precondition is that there must be an actual obligation of confidence. This may arise from an express confidentiality agreement, from an implied obligation based on the circumstances in which the information was provided, or from the nature of the information itself. The Ombudsman assesses this by reference to the established legal tests for breach of confidence: was the information communicated in circumstances importing an obligation of confidence? Does the information have the necessary quality of confidence (that is, it is not trivial or already in the public domain)?

For requesters, the practical limits of this ground are important. An agency cannot create an obligation of confidence simply by labelling information as "confidential" or stamping documents with a confidentiality marking. The substance of the circumstances matters, not the label. Similarly, an agency cannot use a contractual confidentiality clause to override the OIA. The Ombudsman has noted that agencies should not enter into confidentiality obligations that prevent them from meeting their responsibilities under the Act. Where an agency has assumed such an obligation, the Ombudsman will still assess whether the withholding ground is made out on its merits. If the information would not attract protection under the general law of confidence, a contractual provision saying it is confidential does not change that analysis.

Another important limit is that section 9(2)(ba) requires the agency to demonstrate one of the two specified consequences (prejudice to future supply, or damage to the public interest). Simply showing that an obligation of confidence exists is not enough. The agency must show that disclosing the information would cause a specific downstream harm.

Free and Frank Opinions (Section 9(2)(g)(i))

This is one of the most contested grounds in the OIA. It protects the free and frank expression of opinions by officers and employees of any agency, or by Ministers, in the course of their duty. The underlying concern is the "chilling effect": the idea that public disclosure of officials' candid opinions might make them reluctant to express themselves openly and honestly in the future, which would damage the quality of government decision-making.

The Ombudsman's approach to this ground involves a structured analysis that agencies are expected to follow. First, does the information actually contain opinions? The Ombudsman draws a clear distinction between opinions (assessments, evaluations, recommendations, judgments, and advice) and factual or background material (data, descriptions, timelines, and summaries of what happened). Factual information, statistical data, and descriptive background material are not opinions and should not be withheld under this ground. If factual material is intertwined with opinion material, the agency should consider whether it can be separated and the facts released.

Second, would release of the opinions be likely to inhibit the free and frank expression of similar opinions in the future? This is the "chilling effect" question, and the Ombudsman requires a concrete, case-specific assessment, not a general assertion. The Ombudsman considers several factors. The nature and content of the information: early, informal drafts and working papers may warrant more protection than final, considered advice, because people are naturally more tentative and exploratory in early stages of developing their thinking. The context in which it was generated: opinions conveyed informally under pressure of time may be more "free and frank" in nature than polished reports that went through multiple rounds of review. Who generated the information: senior officials are expected to be robust and professional, and are less likely to be deterred by the prospect of disclosure than junior staff or external parties. The Ombudsman has found that senior public servants, who are professionally obligated to provide free and frank advice, would not typically be inhibited by disclosure from continuing to do so. Consultants and lobbyists, whose business depends on providing frank advice regardless of who might see it, are similarly unlikely to be deterred. The relationship between the opinion-holder and their audience matters: if the channel of communication between the parties is one that warrants protection, withholding may be justified to preserve that channel. The timing of the request is critical: if the issue to which the information relates has been concluded, the case for withholding diminishes, and it continues to diminish as time passes.

Third, even if there would be some inhibiting effect, would that inhibition prejudice the effective conduct of public affairs? It is not enough to show that someone might be embarrassed, uncomfortable, or annoyed. The agency must show that the quality of government decision-making would be materially impaired. The Ombudsman has found that information that is detrimental to the effective conduct of public affairs (for example, transcripts revealing poor emergency communications practices) cannot logically be protected under a ground designed to maintain the effective conduct of public affairs.

Research into the OIA's administration has found that free and frank opinions is the ground that generates the most frustration among requesters. There is a widespread perception that agencies invoke it too broadly, applying it to factual material, routine analysis, and considered final advice that does not genuinely require the protection the ground is designed to provide. The Arie research documented that requesters regularly suspect this ground is used to avoid embarrassment or political inconvenience rather than to protect genuine decision-making processes. The Ombudsman shares some of these concerns and has published detailed guidance emphasising the limits of the ground.

For requesters, the most important point is that there is no presumption that disclosure will inhibit candour. The agency must demonstrate, with reference to the specific information and circumstances, that release would have that effect. If an agency cites this ground without explaining how the specific information at issue is genuinely "free and frank" in nature and how its release would genuinely inhibit future candour and thereby prejudice the effective conduct of public affairs, the withholding is vulnerable to challenge. Simply calling something a "draft" does not invoke the protection of section 9(2)(g)(i).

Legal Professional Privilege (Section 9(2)(h))

This ground protects legal professional privilege: the confidentiality of communications between a solicitor and client for the purpose of giving or receiving legal advice (solicitor-client privilege), and communications made in connection with actual or contemplated litigation (litigation privilege). It can also apply to drafting instructions received by the Parliamentary Counsel Office and draft legislation prepared by or on behalf of that office.

The principle underlying legal professional privilege is well-established: people (including government agencies) must be able to seek and receive legal advice in confidence. Without that assurance, the quality and candour of legal advice would suffer, to the detriment of the administration of justice and the rule of law.

For requesters, the practical limits are as follows. The privilege belongs to the client (the agency), not the lawyer. The agency can choose to waive the privilege and release the advice. If the agency has already disclosed the substance of the legal advice in another context (for example, in a public statement or a court filing), the privilege may have been waived. The privilege covers the legal advice itself, not the underlying facts. If you ask for factual information that happens to be mentioned in a legal opinion, the agency may be able to release the facts while withholding the legal analysis and recommendations. The privilege must actually exist: the communication must have been made for the dominant purpose of giving or receiving legal advice or in connection with litigation. Internal discussions that merely mention legal considerations, or reports that happen to be prepared by a lawyer, are not necessarily privileged.

The public interest test applies to this ground, as it does to all section 9 grounds. The Ombudsman has noted that overriding legal professional privilege through the public interest test will be unusual, because the privilege serves a fundamental interest in the administration of justice. But it is not impossible. In one early case, the Ombudsman was prepared to find that legal professional privilege was outweighed by the public interest in disclosure where the circumstances were particularly compelling.

Negotiations (Section 9(2)(j))

This ground protects information where withholding is necessary to enable an agency to carry out, without prejudice or disadvantage, commercial or industrial negotiations. It is forward-looking: it is concerned with protecting the integrity of ongoing or anticipated negotiations, not with shielding completed deals from scrutiny.

For requesters, the key question is whether the negotiations are genuinely ongoing or anticipated. If the negotiations have concluded, the case for withholding under this ground largely evaporates (though other grounds, such as commercial sensitivity under section 9(2)(b), may still apply to the substance of what was negotiated). If the negotiations are ongoing, the agency must show that the specific information at issue would, if released, prejudice or disadvantage its negotiating position. A general claim that release would "undermine" negotiations is not sufficient. The agency must explain, with reference to the specific information, how the other party to the negotiations could use it to gain an advantage.

Disclosure may benefit a negotiating opponent by revealing the agency's strategy, bottom line, or assessment of the other party's position. Disclosure may inhibit a negotiating opponent by revealing information about their position that they would prefer to keep private. In inter-agency negotiations, the analysis is more complex because both parties are subject to the OIA. In contracts of adhesion or compulsory acquisition (where there is no genuine negotiation), the ground may be difficult to establish. The timing distinction between past, present, and future negotiations is important: the ground is designed to protect current or genuinely anticipated future negotiations, not to provide a permanent shield for information about past negotiations.

Confidential Advice to Government (Section 9(2)(f)(iv))

This ground protects the constitutional convention of the confidentiality of advice tendered by Ministers and officials. It usually applies where the release of confidential advice given to Ministers or Cabinet would prejudice the orderly and effective conduct of government decision-making processes.

The ground is designed to preserve a space in which officials can develop and tender advice to Ministers candidly, and in which Ministers can deliberate with each other and with their officials without the process being conducted in real time under public scrutiny. It is closely related to the free and frank opinions ground but is focused specifically on the constitutional relationship between officials and Ministers and the convention that the advisory process leading to government decisions carries a presumption of confidentiality.

For requesters, the practical limits are similar to those for free and frank opinions, with some important differences. The ground is strongest while the relevant decision-making process is still underway. Once a decision has been made and announced, the case for protecting the advice that led to it diminishes significantly. The Ombudsman's guidance notes that accountability considerations are usually strongest after a decision has been made, because the public is then entitled to understand and scrutinise the process. Public participation considerations are usually strongest before a decision, but this is precisely when the risk to the orderly conduct of the process is also highest, making the balancing exercise particularly sensitive.

The ground applies to genuine advice, not to factual or background material that accompanies the advice. It does not protect information simply because it was created within a government department or traversed a Minister's desk. The Ombudsman expects agencies to articulate specifically how the release of the particular information would prejudice the orderly and effective conduct of government decision-making, not simply to assert that the information was part of an advisory process.

Constitutional Conventions (Section 9(2)(f)(i) to (iii))

These grounds protect the constitutional conventions of: the confidentiality of communications by or with the Sovereign or her representative (section 9(2)(f)(i)); collective and individual ministerial responsibility (section 9(2)(f)(ii)); and the political neutrality of officials (section 9(2)(f)(iii)).

Collective ministerial responsibility means that Ministers present a united front on government policy once a Cabinet decision has been made, even if they disagreed in the Cabinet room. The convention allows Ministers to debate issues freely and frankly within Cabinet without fear that their differences will be aired publicly. Information that would reveal the positions taken by individual Ministers in Cabinet discussions, or the nature and extent of disagreement within Cabinet, is the core of what this ground protects.

Individual ministerial responsibility means that Ministers are accountable to Parliament for the actions of their departments. The convention is designed to ensure that Ministers, not officials, face public scrutiny for government decisions. Paradoxically, this convention can sometimes favour disclosure rather than withholding, because accountability requires the public to understand what the Minister is responsible for.

Political neutrality means that officials serve the government of the day impartially and do not become identified with the policies of a particular political party. Information that would reveal the personal political views of officials, or that would identify officials as advocates for a particular political position, may be protected.

These grounds are invoked less frequently than free and frank opinions or confidential advice. The Ombudsman's guidance emphasises that the approach to all section 9(2)(f) grounds follows the same structure: identify the relevant convention, identify its purpose, assess whether release of the information would undermine the convention and explain why, and then consider the public interest in disclosure. A key point from the Eagles, Taggart, and Liddell analysis is that these conventions are means to an end (democratic accountability), not ends in themselves. Where disclosure would actually serve the purposes the conventions are designed to promote (for example, by enhancing accountability), it would be perverse to invoke the conventions to prevent it.

Improper Gain or Advantage (Section 9(2)(k))

This ground is a catch-all, applying where withholding is necessary to prevent the disclosure or use of official information for improper gain or improper advantage. It is rarely invoked and the Ombudsman has given it a narrow interpretation.

The key word is "improper." The gain or advantage must be something more than merely beneficial to the requester. Using government information to make a commercial decision, to inform research, or to hold an agency accountable is not "improper" even if it gives the requester an advantage. The ground is aimed at situations where the information would be used in a way that is dishonest, corrupt, or contrary to the public interest in a direct and identifiable way.

In practice, this ground adds little to the other section 9 protections. Most situations where the ground might apply are already covered by the commercial sensitivity, confidentiality, or negotiations grounds. The Ombudsman has cautioned against treating section 9(2)(k) as a general-purpose withholding ground to be deployed whenever the agency suspects the requester's motives, because the OIA is requester-blind: the identity and purpose of the requester are generally not relevant to the withholding analysis.

Understanding and Challenging the Public Interest Test

If you receive a refusal under section 9 and you believe the public interest favours release, you should articulate the specific public interest factors in any response to the agency or complaint to the Ombudsman. The following framework, drawn from the Ombudsman's public interest guide, provides a structure for doing so.

Start by considering the purpose of your request. If you have a specific reason for wanting the information (for example, to make an informed submission, to pursue a legal remedy, to report on a matter of public concern, or to understand a decision that affects you), state it. The Ombudsman's guidance notes that while requesters are not required to give reasons, voluntarily explaining the purpose can help identify the public interest considerations that favour release.

Then consider the content and context of the information. Information about the expenditure of public money carries a strong accountability interest. Information about a decision-making process that is currently the subject of public consultation carries a strong participation interest. Information about a matter that has generated public controversy or disquiet may carry a strong interest in providing public assurance or correcting misunderstandings. Information about wrongdoing, serious error, or negligence carries a particularly strong public interest in disclosure, because accountability demands that such matters be brought to light.

Consider the stage of the relevant process. If a decision has been made and announced, the accountability interest in understanding how and why it was made is at its strongest, while the need to protect the advisory process is at its weakest. If the process is still underway, the participation interest may be strong (people need information to participate meaningfully), but the agency may have a legitimate interest in protecting the orderly conduct of the process. Making the timing argument explicit can be persuasive.

Consider what is already in the public domain. If some information about the topic has been released (whether by the agency, by proactive release, through media reporting, or through other channels), there may be a public interest in releasing additional information to provide a complete and accurate picture. Selective disclosure that presents only part of the story can be more damaging than full transparency.

Finally, remember that multiple public interest considerations can apply at the same time and their combined weight may be greater than any individual consideration. A request that engages both accountability and participation interests, in the context of a matter that has generated significant public concern, will carry more weight than a request that relies on a single, abstract transparency argument.

Red Flags

The following patterns should alert you to the possibility that the agency has not properly applied section 9. Each is a potential ground for complaint to the Ombudsman.

Bare citation without explanation. The agency has cited a section 9 ground without explaining how it applies to the specific information. A notation of "section 9(2)(g)(i)" beside a redacted passage, without any explanation of why the information constitutes an opinion, why its release would inhibit future candour, or how that inhibition would prejudice the effective conduct of public affairs, is inadequate. The Ombudsman expects agencies to explain their reasoning, not simply cite a provision number.

Blanket claims across a large body of information. Each item of information must be assessed individually. A claim that "all of the withheld information is protected by section 9(2)(g)(i)" without any differentiation between factual material and opinion material, or between early drafts and final advice, suggests the agency has not done the work the Act requires. The Ombudsman has repeatedly emphasised that section 9 grounds must be applied to specific information, not to entire documents or categories of documents as a class.

No mention of the public interest test. For every section 9 ground, the agency must consider the public interest. If the response makes no reference to the public interest, the agency has not completed the required analysis. This is one of the most common deficiencies the Ombudsman identifies in agency decision-making.

Formulaic application of the public interest test. A sentence such as "I have considered the public interest and do not consider it outweighs the need to withhold" without any discussion of the specific factors at play is not a genuine engagement with the test. The Ombudsman expects agencies to identify the specific public interest considerations that apply, assess their weight, and explain why they are or are not sufficient to outweigh the need to withhold.

Factual or background material withheld under free and frank opinions. This ground protects opinions, not facts. If factual data, statistical tables, background descriptions, historical narratives, or summaries of what happened have been redacted under this ground, the agency has likely misapplied it. The Ombudsman has been particularly clear on this point.

Reliance on a time-limited ground after the relevant process has concluded. If negotiations have ended, if the Cabinet decision has been made and announced, or if the policy issue has been resolved, the case for withholding under grounds that protect ongoing processes is significantly weakened. The passage of time should always be considered, and agencies that cite grounds like section 9(2)(j) (negotiations) or section 9(2)(f)(iv) (confidential advice) long after the relevant process has concluded face a heavy burden to explain why withholding is still necessary.

Inconsistency between agencies or over time. If the same type of information has been released by the same agency in response to a previous request, or by a different agency in response to a similar request, an unexplained refusal to release it now raises questions about whether the withholding is genuinely necessary or is instead driven by the specific context of this request. While each request must be assessed on its own merits, inconsistency is a legitimate concern to raise.

Failure to consider partial release. Even where some information within a document warrants protection, the remaining information should be released with appropriate redactions under section 17. An agency that withholds entire documents when only specific passages are sensitive has not complied with its obligation to consider partial release. The Ombudsman regularly finds that documents can be released in part even where full release is not appropriate.

Using section 6 when section 9 would be more appropriate. Section 6 grounds are conclusive (they have no public interest override), while section 9 grounds are subject to the public interest test. If an agency cites section 6 to avoid the public interest test when the information more naturally falls within section 9, this may be a sign that the agency is reaching for a stronger shield than the circumstances warrant. This is a pattern that some requesters and commentators have observed, and it is worth flagging in a complaint.

If you identify one or more of these red flags, you have strong grounds for complaint. Include the specific pattern in your complaint to the Ombudsman, explaining why you believe the withholding ground has been misapplied in the circumstances. The more concrete and specific your explanation, the more effectively the Ombudsman can assess and act on your complaint.

CHAPTER 13

Administrative Reasons for Refusal (Section 18)

The administrative reasons for refusal in section 18 of the OIA (section 17 of LGOIMA) are fundamentally different from the withholding grounds in sections 6 and 9. The conclusive and good reasons for withholding are about protecting substantive interests: security, privacy, commercial sensitivity, the integrity of government decision-making. The administrative grounds are not about protecting interests at all. They are about practical limits on the obligation to provide information. The information might be perfectly harmless, but the agency cannot provide it because it does not hold it, because finding it would require too much work, because another statute forbids disclosure, or because the request itself is an abuse of the right.

This distinction matters for requesters because it affects your strategy. When an agency refuses on substantive grounds, the argument is about whether the harm from disclosure outweighs the public interest in release. When an agency refuses on administrative grounds, the argument is about whether the agency has done its homework: has it searched properly, considered the alternatives, and met the procedural requirements that the Act imposes before an administrative refusal can be made?

Administrative reasons are not subject to the public interest test. This means that if an administrative ground genuinely applies, there is no override based on the public interest in disclosure. However, reliance on these grounds is discretionary: an agency may still choose to provide information even if an administrative ground is available. This will usually be in cases where the agency recognises that the information should be readily accessible, even though it is not, or because there is a clear and compelling public interest in release. The Ombudsman will scrutinise whether the agency has met the preconditions for relying on each ground before accepting that the refusal is justified.

Information Not Held (Sections 18(e) and 18(g))

Two provisions deal with the situation where the agency does not have the information you asked for.

Section 18(e) applies where the document alleged to contain the information does not exist, or cannot be found despite reasonable efforts to locate it. This covers two different scenarios: the document was never created, or it was created but has been lost, destroyed, or misfiled.

Section 18(g) applies more broadly where the information is not held by the agency and there are no grounds for believing it is held by, or more closely connected with the functions of, another agency. This covers situations where the information would need to be created (rather than extracted or compiled from existing records), where the information is not held in the agency's official capacity, and where the information falls within the specific exclusions from the definition of "official information" (such as library material held solely for reference or exhibition purposes, or correspondence with the Ombudsman in relation to investigations).

The distinction between creation and collation is important. There is no obligation under the OIA to create new information in order to respond to a request. But the line between creating information and compiling information that already exists is not always clear. If the information is already held in various locations and simply needs to be gathered together, that is collation (and the relevant ground, if the work is substantial, is section 18(f), not section 18(g)). If responding to the request would require the application of complex skill, judgment, or interpretation to produce something fundamentally different from what is already held, that is creation, and the agency can refuse under section 18(g). The Ombudsman may seek independent technical advice to determine which side of the line a particular request falls on.

Before relying on either section 18(e) or 18(g), the agency must meet certain requirements that are important for requesters to understand.

For section 18(e), the agency must make a reasonable search. The Ombudsman's guidance makes clear that a reasonable search must be thorough and intelligent, not mechanical or perfunctory. It should involve asking relevant staff to search their files and systems and to confirm the outcome; searching physical filing systems; searching email accounts, shared drives, document management systems, business systems, databases, and other electronic repositories (with searches by a user with administrative rights being more comprehensive than those by a general user); consulting information management staff about how to find the information and any disposal actions that may have been taken; and consulting IT staff about whether deleted information can reasonably be recovered.

The agency does not need to leave no stone unturned, but it must follow all obvious lines of inquiry and have convincing reasons for concluding that the document does not exist or cannot be found. A "desultory attempt" at searching will not satisfy the Ombudsman. The agency should keep full records of its searches, including the name and function of each system searched, the search terms used, which staff were involved, and the outcome. Screenshots of electronic searches can be helpful. These records will be critical if you complain and the Ombudsman needs to assess the adequacy of the search.

Where information has been destroyed in accordance with a proper disposal authority under the Public Records Act 2005, the agency will not usually need to try to recover it from backup systems. But where information has been disposed of without proper authority, the agency may need to make additional efforts, including searching backup systems.

For both provisions, the agency should consider consulting you before refusing. The Ombudsman expects agencies to explain the difficulty to the requester, describe what information is held, and ask whether the requester can suggest additional search locations, alternative search terms, or a revised request. Requesters who have been given this opportunity are less likely to complain to the Ombudsman, and the consultation often produces practical results: you may be able to point the agency towards systems or staff it has not yet checked, or you may be willing to accept related information that the agency does hold.

The agency must also consider whether any of the information should be transferred to another agency. If the agency has grounds for believing the information is held by, or more closely connected with the functions of, another agency, it must transfer the request rather than simply refusing.

One further point: information is "held" even if it is incomplete or inaccurate. The fact that information is imperfect does not justify a refusal under section 18(g). The right of access is to information that is held, not to information that is accurate. If the agency holds relevant information but it is incomplete, the proper course is to release it with a contextual statement explaining the limitations.

If you receive a "not held" response and you believe the information should exist, ask the agency to explain what searches it conducted, which staff were asked, what systems were checked, and what search terms were used. If the agency's record-keeping failures are the reason the information cannot be found, the Ombudsman has held that the agency cannot rely on its own administrative failings to justify a refusal. In one notable case involving the Department of Corrections, the Chief Ombudsman found that the department should have been keeping centralised records of alleged staff assaults under its own Prison Operations Manual. The required notification forms existed; the department simply had not been following its own procedures. The Chief Ombudsman did not accept that substantial collation or research applied either, because the difficulty was down to the department's own administrative lapses. The department agreed to collate and release what it could find, and to change its practices going forward. In another case, the Police could not find their report on the Cave Creek tragedy, and reasonable efforts included asking the Commissioner of the Cave Creek Inquiry, counsel assisting the Commission, and searching records at the Crown Law Office.

Substantial Collation or Research (Section 18(f))

Section 18(f) provides that a request may be refused if the information requested cannot be made available without substantial collation or research. This is about the physical accessibility of the information: how much work would be required to find it and bring it together.

"Research" means finding the information. "Collation" means bringing it together. Both terms refer to the labour involved in locating and assembling the requested material, not the labour involved in deciding whether to release it.

This distinction is critical and often misunderstood. Decision-making time does not count towards the assessment of whether collation or research is "substantial." The Ombudsman's guidance is explicit: the time required for reading, reviewing, and assessing the information for release; for consulting third parties or legal advisors about withholding; and for redacting information that the agency has decided to withhold are all part of the decision-making process, not part of the collation or research. As the High Court noted in one case, making a decision on an OIA request requires each piece of information to be assessed against the criteria for withholding, and while that may involve substantial effort, that is the price Parliament contemplated when it passed the Act.

Similarly, the time required to present information in the agency's preferred format, draft cover letters, prepare briefings to Ministers, or conduct internal quality assurance and sign-off processes cannot count towards establishing substantial collation or research. These are tasks done after the information has been found and brought together, on the agency's initiative, as a matter of its own internal processes.

Whether the collation or research is "substantial" depends on the circumstances. The Ombudsman considers factors including the quantity of information involved, the amount of time required to locate and assemble it, the number of staff who would need to be diverted from their regular duties, the impact on the agency's other operations (including its ability to respond to other OIA requests), and the nature and size of the agency. There is no fixed threshold. In one case, manually reviewing up to 150,000 immigration applications to extract medical waiver statistics was accepted as substantial. In another, the Minister of Finance's refusal of a request for 20 Treasury reports on grounds of substantial collation or research was overturned because the work involved was consultation, not collation.

Where the difficulty in providing the information is the agency's own fault, the Ombudsman may find it unreasonable for the agency to rely on section 18(f). If an agency has failed to organise its records properly, or has not been following its own record-keeping protocols, the Ombudsman may expect the agency to bear that burden rather than pass it to the requester. The Ombudsman has also noted that agencies should be able to release information in its existing form, along with a contextual statement about limitations on its accuracy or completeness, rather than refusing because the information is not in a polished state. The desire to verify or guarantee accuracy does not justify a refusal when the information is already held.

What makes section 18(f) critical for requesters is the set of mandatory preconditions that the agency must meet before relying on this ground. The Act requires the agency to consider three alternatives before refusing.

First, the agency must genuinely consider charging. Could it meet the request if it charged you for the work involved? Charging can be particularly helpful where the work can be done by anyone and additional staff can be hired or redeployed. It may not help if the work requires a specialist whose diversion would significantly harm the agency's operations, or if the requester is unable or unwilling to pay. But agencies should not simply assume that the requester will not pay; the Ombudsman's guidance suggests they should ask.

Second, the agency must genuinely consider extending the time limit. Could it do the work if it had longer? An extension allows the agency to spread the work over time, fitting it in alongside other responsibilities. This works particularly well when the workload pressures the agency faces are expected to ease, or when additional resources are expected to become available.

Third, the agency must consider consulting you. The Law Commission stated in its 2012 review that it is unreasonable for an agency to refuse a request outright under section 18(f) if it has made no effort to discuss the matter with the requester. The Ombudsman will in most cases expect the agency to have made reasonable efforts to consult before refusing. The purpose of consultation is to help you make the request in a way that would not require substantial collation or research.

The agency should explain the specific volume of information involved, the estimated time required, and the impact on its operations. With that information, you may be willing to accept one or more practical solutions. These include: narrowing the request by date range, subject matter, or document type; accepting a subset or sample of the information rather than the full set; accepting other information that is already to hand or easily extracted (such as data already compiled for a select committee or extracted from a financial system); accepting the information in an alternative form, such as by inspection, summary, or excerpt; accepting release on conditions (for example, receiving unredacted information on condition that it not be published); or prioritising parts of the request and accepting release in stages.

In one case involving requests for details of expenditure on contractors and consultants from three agencies, all three agencies initially refused on grounds of substantial collation or research. The Ombudsman investigated, and the complaints were resolved by the agencies agreeing to provide information already compiled for select committees, along with data easily extracted from their financial systems, with appropriate caveats about what the information did and did not include. In another case involving a request for details of 404 land covenants, the Department of Conservation could not search all 13 conservancy offices, but was able to provide a report of readily extracted information from its Land Register, which the requester could then use to make more specific follow-up requests. Both cases illustrate that creative engagement with the requester can produce a result even when the full request is genuinely too large.

If the agency refuses under section 18(f) without genuinely considering all three alternatives, the refusal is vulnerable to challenge. An agency that simply tells you the request is too big, without engaging with the alternatives, has not met the statutory requirements.

Contrary to an Enactment (Section 18(c)(i))

Section 18(c)(i) provides that a request may be refused if making the information available would be contrary to the provisions of a specified enactment. This ground applies where another statute controls the availability of the information and releasing it under the OIA would breach that statute.

The most commonly encountered example is section 81 of the Tax Administration Act 1994, which requires the Inland Revenue Department to maintain secrecy regarding taxation matters. Because section 81 controls the availability of tax information, the OIA does not override it, and a request for such information can be refused under section 18(c)(i). However, even section 81 contains exceptions: the Commissioner has discretion to release information about a person's own taxation matters if satisfied the information is readily available and it is reasonable and practicable to provide it.

Other enactments that may restrict disclosure include provisions in the Statistics Act (protecting the confidentiality of census and survey data), the Health Act (restricting disclosure of certain health information), and various regulatory statutes that impose specific confidentiality obligations on particular types of information.

When an agency relies on section 18(c)(i), it must identify the specific enactment and the specific provision it is relying on. A bare assertion that disclosure would be "contrary to law" without identifying the statute is not sufficient. You are entitled to know which enactment is said to prevent disclosure, and you can then assess for yourself whether the provision actually applies to the information you requested.

Three points are important for requesters. First, the other enactment must actually prohibit disclosure. If the enactment confers a discretion (allowing but not requiring disclosure in certain circumstances), the agency should consider exercising that discretion in your favour. Second, even if the enactment prohibits disclosure of some of the information, the agency should still consider whether any of the remaining information can be released under the OIA. Third, section 18(c)(i) is about genuinely conflicting statutory obligations, not about convenience. An agency cannot use this ground simply because another statute creates a confidentiality regime that the agency would prefer to follow; the other statute must actually make release under the OIA unlawful.

Contempt of Court or the House (Section 18(c)(ii))

Section 18(c)(ii) provides that a request may be refused if making the information available would constitute contempt of court or contempt of the House of Representatives. Section 52(1) of the OIA reinforces this by providing that nothing in the Act authorises or permits disclosure if that disclosure would constitute contempt of court or of the House.

Contempt of court is about preserving the administration of justice. It may consist of words or acts that obstruct or interfere with the courts, or disobedience of court orders. In the OIA context, the most common applications are where information is the subject of a suppression order, where disclosure might breach an injunction, or where a Coroner has prohibited the publication of evidence given at an inquest. If a court has ordered that certain information be suppressed, releasing it in response to an OIA request would breach that order and constitute contempt.

Contempt of the House of Representatives is about protecting Parliament's ability to function. The Standing Orders define contempt broadly as any act or omission that obstructs or impedes the House, its members, or its officers, or that has a tendency to produce such results. In the OIA context, the most common applications involve select committee proceedings. Divulging the proceedings of a select committee before it has reported to the House, disclosing a committee's report or draft report before it has been presented, or releasing evidence that a committee has declared secret would likely constitute contempt.

Draft answers to parliamentary questions held by agencies also raise these issues. The Ombudsman has considered several cases involving requests for draft answers to parliamentary questions and has found that section 18(c)(ii) may apply, though in practice such information is more commonly withheld under section 9(2)(f)(iv) (confidential advice to government).

For requesters, section 18(c)(ii) is a relatively narrow ground. The test is demanding: the disclosure "would constitute" contempt, not merely "might." The Eagles, Taggart and Liddell analysis notes that because the determination of whether the House would regard material as contemptuous is inherently problematic, the better view is that information which only might be regarded as a contempt should not be withheld on this ground. If you receive a refusal citing section 18(c)(ii), check whether the agency has identified the specific basis for the contempt: a court order, a Standing Order, or an established form of contempt. If the agency's reasoning is vague, ask for specifics. The Ombudsman's guidance notes that where it is not clear that release would constitute contempt of the House, agencies should consult the Office of the Clerk before relying on this ground.

Also consider whether some of the requested information could be released without constituting contempt. Even if part of the information is caught by a suppression order or relates to confidential committee proceedings, other parts of the request may be unaffected and should be considered for release.

Soon to Be Publicly Available (Section 18(d))

Section 18(d) provides that a request may be refused if the information is or will soon be publicly available. The purpose of this ground is practical: there is no point in the agency going through the full OIA process if the same information is about to be published through normal channels.

The Ombudsman's guidance makes clear that for section 18(d) to apply, two conditions must be met. The agency must be reasonably certain that the requested information will be published, and the publication must be in the near future. A vague intention to publish at some unspecified time is not sufficient. The Ombudsman has distinguished section 18(d) from the situation where an agency's real concern is that premature disclosure would harm a substantive interest protected by sections 6 or 9. If the agency is worried about the timing of disclosure because of the harm early release might cause (for example, to an ongoing negotiation or an upcoming policy announcement), the appropriate route is to refuse under the relevant substantive ground, not to rely on section 18(d).

For requesters, the issues with this ground are timing and certainty. Agencies sometimes claim that information will be published "soon" without specifying when, or cite plans for publication that are vague or subject to change. If you receive a refusal citing section 18(d), ask the agency to specify when the information will be publicly available, in what form, and where it will be accessible. If the timeframe is unreasonably long or uncertain, challenge the refusal. The Ombudsman will assess whether the agency's claim about the timing and certainty of publication is reasonable.

One further point: if the information is already publicly available, the agency should tell you where to find it rather than simply refusing. Good practice is to provide the specific URL or location. If the proactively released version is incomplete or redacted, you can still request the full version under the OIA, and the fact that a partial version has been published does not justify refusing to provide the complete information.

Frivolous, Vexatious, or Trivial (Section 18(h))

Section 18(h) provides that a request may be refused if it is frivolous or vexatious, or if the information requested is trivial. This ground exists to protect agencies from requests that amount to an abuse of the right to access official information.

The threshold for invoking section 18(h) is high. The Ombudsman has consistently emphasised that requesters should not be unfairly denied the opportunity to make genuine requests, and that section 18(h) provides a necessary but narrow power.

A request is frivolous if it has no serious purpose or value. A request is vexatious if it is made to harass or annoy, or is part of a pattern of conduct designed to disrupt the agency's operations rather than to obtain information for a legitimate purpose. The Ombudsman has confirmed that a request can properly be described as vexatious when it amounts to an abuse of the right to make a request, rather than a legitimate exercise of that right. It is not enough that the request has disturbed, troubled, or annoyed the agency. It must carry overtones of impropriety, and such overtones may be found in the surrounding circumstances or the history of the relationship between the parties. Information is trivial if it is of such minor significance that the effort of processing the request would be disproportionate to any conceivable value in the information.

Making a large number of requests, by itself, does not make any individual request vexatious. The Ombudsman looks at the nature of the specific request in the context of the surrounding circumstances. Factors that may support a finding of vexatiousness include: requests made solely to harass or annoy staff; requests that are part of a broader campaign of disruptive conduct; requests for information the requester already has and does not need again; requests that appear designed to challenge the competence or integrity of individual officials rather than to obtain useful information; and requests framed in aggressive, offensive, or threatening language.

Factors that weigh against a finding of vexatiousness include: the requester has a legitimate interest in the information; the requester's underlying grievance is to some extent justified; the agency's own handling of earlier requests has contributed to the current difficulties (in which case the agency should be expected to absorb more of the burden); and the information has genuine value to the requester or the public.

The Ombudsman has also noted that a repeat request on the same subject is not the same as a repeat request for the same information. Agencies must be satisfied that the request is in fact for the same information sought previously, not merely that it is about the same topic or similarly worded. To the extent that different information is captured, the request cannot reasonably be regarded as a repeat. If the same information has already been supplied, the better course may be to explain this to the requester and confirm that no additional relevant information is held, rather than refusing as vexatious. A request for information in a different format (for example, in electronic form after receiving it on paper) is a new request and should be assessed on its merits.

Before refusing a request under section 18(h), the Ombudsman expects agencies to have considered whether any other provisions are more appropriate (such as section 18(f) for large requests, or section 9(2)(g)(ii) for requests that involve improper pressure on staff). Agencies should also warn the requester before resorting to section 18(h) and give them an opportunity to reframe the request, particularly where the concern is about offensive or aggressive language rather than the substance of what is being asked. If the requester refuses to moderate their behaviour after being warned, the agency's position is strengthened. If the agency never raised its concerns, its case for refusing as vexatious is weakened.

Your Right to Challenge Any Administrative Refusal

All administrative refusals under section 18 are reviewable by the Ombudsman. Your complaint should be tailored to the specific ground the agency relied on.

If the agency refused on the basis that information is not held, ask what searches were conducted and provide any information that might help the Ombudsman assess the adequacy of those searches. If you know of specific places the agency may not have looked, say so. If you believe the agency should hold the information under its own record-keeping obligations, explain why. The Ombudsman can also notify the Chief Archivist if a complaint raises concerns about an agency's compliance with the Public Records Act 2005.

If the agency refused on the basis of substantial collation or research, ask whether the agency considered charging, extending, and consulting you. If it did not, this is a strong basis for a complaint. If it did, ask for the specifics of the work involved and challenge any estimates that include decision-making time, internal sign-off processes, or presentation work that should not count. Point out any creative alternatives (subsets, samples, alternative formats, phased release) that the agency does not appear to have considered.

If the agency refused on the basis of another enactment, ask the Ombudsman to review whether the enactment actually prohibits disclosure of the specific information at issue, whether the agency considered exercising any discretion the other enactment may confer, and whether some of the information could still be released under the OIA.

If the agency refused on the basis that information will soon be publicly available, ask the Ombudsman to assess whether the agency's claim about timing and certainty is reasonable. If the publication date is vague or distant, the ground should not apply.

If the agency refused on the basis that your request is frivolous or vexatious, explain the legitimate purpose behind your request, point to any history of the agency's own failings in handling your earlier requests, and emphasise that frequency alone does not equal vexatiousness.

In every case, remember that the principle of availability underpins the entire Act. Administrative grounds are not about protecting interests; they are about practical limits. The Ombudsman will expect agencies to have made genuine efforts to find ways to meet your request before resorting to refusal. A refusal that comes without evidence of real engagement with the alternatives is a refusal that is ripe for challenge.

PART FIVE

WHEN THINGS GO WRONG

CHAPTER 14

Complaining to the Ombudsman

The Ombudsman is the cornerstone of the OIA system. Without independent review, the principle of availability would be little more than a statement of aspiration. It is the availability of the Ombudsman as an accessible, free, and independent reviewer that gives the Act its practical force. This chapter explains how the complaint process works, what you can expect, and how to use it effectively.

Your Right to Complain: What the Ombudsman Can Investigate

Section 28 of the OIA sets out the Ombudsman's functions in relation to requests for official information. The scope of what the Ombudsman can investigate is broad. It covers every significant decision an agency makes in response to your request.

The Ombudsman can investigate refusals to make official information available. This includes both express refusals (where the agency tells you it is withholding information and gives its reasons) and partial refusals (where the agency releases some information but withholds the rest). It also includes what are sometimes called "deemed refusals": if an agency fails to respond to your request within the statutory time limit of 20 working days (or within an extended time limit that has been validly notified), that failure is treated as a refusal for the purposes of the complaint process. Similarly, undue delay in making information available after a decision has been made is deemed to be a refusal. You do not need to wait for a formal letter of refusal before you can complain.

The Ombudsman can investigate delays in making a decision or releasing information. This covers both the failure to make a decision within the statutory time limit and the failure to release information promptly after the decision has been made. The Act requires agencies to make their decision "as soon as reasonably practicable" and no later than 20 working days after receiving the request. If the agency is late, you can complain.

The Ombudsman can investigate extensions of time. If an agency extends the 20-working-day time limit under section 15A, you have the right to complain about that extension. The Ombudsman can review whether the extension was made on valid statutory grounds, whether it was notified within the original time limit, and whether the extended period is reasonable in the circumstances.

The Ombudsman can investigate decisions about charges. If you are charged for the supply of official information, and you believe the charge is unreasonable or improperly calculated, you can complain. The Ombudsman will assess the charge against the Government's Charging Guidelines and the Ombudsman's own guidance on what can and cannot be charged for.

The Ombudsman can investigate decisions about the manner of release. This includes decisions about the format in which information is provided (for example, if you asked for electronic copies but were given paper, or if you asked for copies but were only offered an opportunity to inspect), and any conditions imposed on the use, communication, or publication of information that has been released to you.

The Ombudsman can investigate refusals to confirm or deny the existence of information. Section 10 of the OIA allows agencies, in limited circumstances, to refuse to confirm or deny whether information exists. If you receive a section 10 response and you believe it is unjustified, you can complain.

There are a few things the Ombudsman cannot investigate under section 28. The OIA does not give the Ombudsman express authority to investigate complaints about the transfer of a request from one agency to another, or about an agency's failure to respond with the urgency you requested. However, the Ombudsman may be able to investigate these matters under the general jurisdiction of the Ombudsmen Act 1975, which covers complaints about administrative conduct by government agencies.

How to Make a Complaint: The Process in Practice

Making a complaint to the Ombudsman is straightforward. There is no special form, no legal requirement to cite particular provisions, and no fee.

The complaint must be in writing. You can email the Office of the Ombudsman at info@ombudsman.parliament.nz, write to PO Box 10152, Wellington 6143, or use the complaint form on the Ombudsman's website. While the Act also permits oral complaints, these must be put in writing as soon as practicable, so it is simplest to start in writing.

What to include in your complaint: at a minimum, you should provide a copy of your original request (or a description of it, including the date), a copy of the agency's response (or an explanation that no response was received), and an explanation of what you disagree with and why. The more specific you can be about the issues, the easier it will be for the Ombudsman's staff to assess your complaint and begin work on it.

You do not need to make a legal argument. You do not need to cite sections of the Act or explain how the withholding grounds should be applied. The Ombudsman will form an independent view on the merits of the agency's decision. But if you have particular knowledge or arguments that you think are relevant (for example, if you know that similar information has previously been released, or if you can point to specific public interest factors that favour release), it is helpful to include them.

A few practical points. First, you should complain promptly. There is no strict time limit for making a complaint, but the Ombudsman may decline to investigate if the matter is more than 12 months old. Second, keep copies of everything you send to the Ombudsman, including your original request, the agency's response, and your complaint itself. Third, if your complaint involves multiple issues (for example, both a refusal and a charge), explain each issue separately. This helps the Ombudsman's staff to assess and prioritise the different elements of your complaint.

What Happens After You Complain

The complaint process has several stages, and it is useful to understand what happens at each one.

Preliminary assessment

When the Ombudsman's office receives your complaint, a staff member will review it to determine whether it falls within the Ombudsman's jurisdiction and whether there is a valid ground of complaint. At this stage, the

Ombudsman may seek further clarification from you to understand the issues more clearly. The Ombudsman will also consider whether there are grounds to decline the complaint (discussed below).

Informal resolution

In many cases, particularly those involving delays or straightforward disagreements, the Ombudsman's staff will make informal enquiries with the agency to see whether the matter can be resolved without a formal investigation. This might involve a phone call or email to the agency, drawing attention to the complaint and asking the agency to reconsider its position or to provide a response that has been overdue.

This informal approach is remarkably effective. Research into the operation of the OIA has found that many complaints are resolved during the preliminary or informal stages, without the need for a formal investigation. The mere fact of an enquiry from the Ombudsman's office often focuses the agency's attention and produces results. Commentators on the system have noted that the Ombudsman's informal triage approach allows many smaller issues to be resolved quickly, reserving formal investigations for the cases that genuinely require them.

Formal investigation

If the complaint cannot be resolved informally, and the Ombudsman decides to investigate, the agency will be formally notified. The notification will convey the substance of your complaint and ask the agency to provide a report setting out its reasons for the decision. Where information has been withheld, the Ombudsman will ask the agency to provide a copy of the withheld information so that the Ombudsman can review it directly.

At this stage, the Ombudsman has not formed any view on the merits of the complaint. The notification is simply the start of the formal process.

The investigation process

The Ombudsman's investigation is inquisitorial, not adversarial. The Ombudsman is not acting as your advocate or the agency's defender. The Ombudsman is conducting an independent inquiry into whether the agency's decision was correct.

The investigation typically proceeds as follows. The agency provides its report, explaining the reasons for its decision and the grounds it relied on.

The Ombudsman reviews the withheld information (the Ombudsman has the power to see all information that has been withheld, regardless of the grounds cited). The Ombudsman considers the agency's arguments, your submissions, and the applicable law. If the withholding was based on section 9(2)(a) (privacy), the Ombudsman must consult with the Privacy Commissioner before forming a final opinion on the merits of that ground.

After considering all the material, the Ombudsman forms a provisional view. If the provisional view is that the information was properly withheld, the Ombudsman will write to you explaining the reasoning and giving you an opportunity to make further submissions before any final view is formed. If, after considering your submissions, the Ombudsman remains of the view that the information was properly withheld, the investigation will be concluded on that basis.

If the Ombudsman's provisional view is that the information should not have been withheld, the Ombudsman will write to the agency explaining the reasoning and giving the agency an opportunity to respond. In many cases, agencies choose to release the information at this point rather than continue to defend their position. If the agency does not agree to release, and the Ombudsman remains of the view that the information should be released after considering the agency's response, the process moves to a formal recommendation.

The provisional opinion stage is important. It is your main opportunity to put your arguments before the Ombudsman and to respond to the agency's reasons. If you receive a provisional view that is unfavourable, take it seriously. Read the reasoning carefully, and if you have additional arguments or information that might change the Ombudsman's view, submit them promptly.

The Ombudsman's final opinion and recommendation

If the Ombudsman concludes that the request should not have been refused, or that the decision was unreasonable or wrong, the Ombudsman will report that opinion with reasons to the agency, and will make such recommendations as the Ombudsman thinks fit. A copy of the recommendation will also be sent to you.

The most common recommendation is that the agency release the information that was withheld. But the Ombudsman can also recommend other remedial action, depending on the nature of the complaint.

Once a recommendation is made, a public duty to observe that recommendation is imposed on the agency from the 21st working day after the day on which the recommendation was made. This means the recommendation becomes legally binding unless the executive override (discussed below) is invoked before that 21st day.

When the Ombudsman May Decline to Investigate

The Ombudsman is not required to investigate every complaint. Under section 17 of the Ombudsmen Act 1975, the Ombudsman may decline to investigate in the following circumstances.

First, if there is an adequate remedy or right of appeal to which it would have been reasonable for the complainant to resort. This might apply if another statutory process (such as the Privacy Act complaint process) would be a more appropriate avenue for the particular issue.

Second, if the complainant has known about the matter for more than 12 months. This is a discretionary ground, not an absolute bar, but it means you should not delay unnecessarily before complaining.

Third, if the subject matter of the complaint is trivial.

Fourth, if the complaint is frivolous or vexatious or is not made in good faith.

Fifth, if the complainant does not have a sufficient personal interest in the subject matter of the complaint.

In practice, the Ombudsman declines to investigate only in clear cases. The discretion is exercised cautiously, because the Ombudsman recognises that the complaint process is the primary mechanism for enforcing the OIA. If the Ombudsman declines your complaint, you will be informed of the reasons.

Timeframes: How Long Investigations Take in Practice

There is no statutory time limit for the Ombudsman to complete an investigation, and the time taken varies significantly depending on the complexity of the issues, the volume of withheld information to be reviewed, and the Ombudsman's overall caseload.

Simple complaints, particularly those involving delays or clear-cut issues, may be resolved within weeks through the informal enquiry process. More complex investigations, involving contested withholding grounds, large volumes of information, and multiple rounds of submissions from both parties, can take many months. Some investigations have taken more than a year.

Research into the Act's administration has consistently identified the length of the complaint process as one of its most significant weaknesses from the requester's perspective. Many requesters have expressed frustration that by the time a complaint is resolved, the information has lost much of its value, particularly for journalists and others seeking information about current events or policy debates. Some have described being told by the Ombudsman's office to prioritise their complaints because the office could not deal with all of them quickly.

The volume of complaints has grown substantially over the life of the Act. During Chief Ombudsman Peter Boshier's tenure from 2015 to 2025, the total number of complaints received by the Ombudsman's office increased by 110 percent. This growth has inevitably put pressure on the office's capacity to resolve complaints quickly.

There are a few things you can do to manage the timeframe issue. If your complaint involves an element of genuine urgency (for example, if the information is needed for a submission deadline, a court proceeding, or a time-sensitive public interest matter), say so in your complaint and explain the reasons for urgency. The Ombudsman has the ability to prioritise complaints, and a clear case for urgency may lead to faster action. You should also respond promptly to any correspondence from the Ombudsman's office, because delays on your side will add to the overall timeline.

Be realistic about what the process can deliver. For time-sensitive matters, the Ombudsman's informal enquiry process is your best hope for a quick result. For complex withholding disputes, the investigation will take time, but the thoroughness of the process is what makes the Ombudsman's opinions authoritative and effective.

The Limits of the Ombudsman's Power: Recommendations, Not Orders

The Ombudsman's power under the OIA is recommendatory, not determinative. The Ombudsman investigates, forms an opinion, and makes a recommendation. The Ombudsman does not order the release of information. It is the agency that releases the information, in compliance with the Ombudsman's recommendation.

However, the Ombudsman's recommendations have legal force in a way that is unusual for an Ombudsman institution. Under section 32 of the OIA, once the Ombudsman makes a recommendation, a public duty to observe that recommendation is imposed on the agency from the 21st working day after the day on which the recommendation was made. If the agency fails to comply, the Ombudsman can report the failure to the Prime Minister, and can thereafter make a report to the House of Representatives. These reporting powers give the Ombudsman significant practical leverage, because a report to Parliament on an agency's refusal to comply with an Ombudsman's recommendation is a serious matter that attracts public attention and political consequences.

The executive override

The only way an agency can avoid complying with the Ombudsman's recommendation is through the executive override. In the case of the OIA, this requires an Order in Council: a formal decision of the Governor-General acting on the advice of the Executive Council (effectively, a Cabinet decision). The Order in Council must be made before the 21st working day after the recommendation, must set out the reasons for the decision and the grounds in support of it, and must be published in the New Zealand Gazette.

In the case of LGOIMA, the equivalent mechanism is a resolution of the local authority, recorded in writing.

The executive override was a central element of the Danks Committee's original design. The committee believed that decisions on the release of government information should ultimately rest with elected representatives, and that it was important to preserve the Ombudsman's traditional role as a recommender rather than a decision-maker. The original OIA gave the override power to individual Ministers. However, concerns that this power was being used too readily led to the 1987 amendment that elevated it to a collective Cabinet decision requiring an Order in Council.

Since that change was made, the power has never been used. Research into the Act's administration has found that most people involved in the system consider the veto to be effectively unusable. The reasons are partly political (invoking the override would draw enormous public attention to the information in question and would be seen as a direct challenge to the Ombudsman's authority) and partly constitutional (there is a widespread view that formally overriding the Ombudsman would be seen as constitutionally explosive, and could provoke the Ombudsman to resign in protest or make a damaging report to Parliament).

Nonetheless, those who have worked in senior government positions have suggested that the veto power remains relevant as a background factor. It continues to be raised in discussions between the Ombudsman and Ministers when significant issues are at stake. It operates, in the view of these participants, as a reserve power: its influence comes from the possibility of its use, not from its actual exercise.

For requesters, the practical significance of all this is straightforward. Once the Ombudsman recommends that information be released, the agency will almost certainly comply. The executive override exists in theory but has not been used in nearly four decades. The Ombudsman's recommendation is, in practice, the final word.

Tips for Effective Complaints

Drawing together the advice from this chapter, here are several practical tips for making the complaint process work as effectively as possible.

Complain promptly. The sooner you complain after receiving an unsatisfactory response (or after the time limit has passed without a response), the sooner the Ombudsman can begin work. Delay reduces the value of the information and may weaken your position.

Be specific about what you are complaining about. If you disagree with a particular withholding ground, say so and explain why. If you are complaining about delay, identify the dates. If you are complaining about a charge, explain which aspects you consider unreasonable. The more focused your complaint, the more efficiently the Ombudsman can deal with it.

Provide all relevant documentation. Include your original request, the agency's response (including any extension notices, charge notifications, or other correspondence), and any follow-up communications between you and the agency. If you spoke to the agency by phone, include any email confirmation of those conversations. The Ombudsman's staff should not have to ask you for material that you could have provided at the outset.

Explain the public interest if it is relevant. If you believe there is a strong public interest in the release of the information, say so and explain the specific factors. The Ombudsman will conduct the public interest test independently, but your submissions can draw attention to considerations that might otherwise be overlooked.

Respond promptly to the Ombudsman's correspondence. If the Ombudsman asks you for further information or gives you an opportunity to comment on a provisional view, respond as quickly as you can. Delays in your responses will add to the overall timeline.

Be realistic about timeframes. Simple complaints may be resolved quickly through informal enquiries. Complex investigations will take longer. If urgency is a factor, explain why and ask the Ombudsman to prioritise, but understand that the office has a large caseload and cannot fast-track every complaint.

Prioritise the issues that matter most to you. If your complaint involves multiple issues, identify the ones that are most important to you. This helps the Ombudsman allocate resources effectively and may enable the most important elements to be dealt with first.

Stay engaged throughout the process. The complaint process works best when both parties are responsive and constructive. Check your email regularly for correspondence from the Ombudsman's office. If you have new information or arguments that become relevant during the investigation, provide them. If the agency releases some information during the investigation, let the Ombudsman know whether that resolves part or all of your complaint.

Remember that the Ombudsman is independent. The Ombudsman is not your advocate. The investigation is an impartial inquiry into whether the agency's decision was correct. You may not always get the result you want. But the process is fair, thorough, and free, and it is the most effective mechanism available for holding agencies to account under the OIA. Use it whenever you have a legitimate grievance, and use it well.

CHAPTER 15

Going to Court

The Ombudsman is the primary remedy for OIA disputes, and for most requesters, the Ombudsman process will be both the beginning and the end of the story. But the courts have a role too, and understanding that role, even if you never need to use it, helps you see the full picture of how the system works.

The Limited Role of the Courts under the OIA

The Danks Committee and the legislature deliberately preferred the Ombudsman to the courts as the dispute-resolving body under the OIA. The reasons were pragmatic. The Ombudsman's investigation is informal, inquisitorial, wide-ranging, and free of charge. Court proceedings are adversarial, formal, expensive, and slow. For a system designed to make official information accessible to ordinary citizens, the Ombudsman was clearly the better fit.

The result is that the courts have what the Eagles/Taggart/Liddell text describes as "an important but reserve role" under the Act. The courts do not routinely hear OIA disputes. They enter the picture only in specific, limited circumstances. Most requesters will never need to go to court, and the chapter that follows is included for completeness and for the small number of cases where court involvement becomes necessary or worth considering.

When You Can Go to Court: After the Ombudsman Has Determined Your Complaint

If you are seeking official information under Part 2 of the OIA and an agency refuses your request, section 34 imposes a significant restriction on your ability to go to court. You cannot make an application for judicial review of the refusal, or commence any proceedings challenging the decision, until you have first complained to the Ombudsman and the complaint has been "determined" under the Act.

This is not a complete exclusion of judicial review. It is a postponement. The legislature's intention was clear: it wanted requesters to exhaust the Ombudsman process first, and only then to turn to the courts if necessary. Given that the Ombudsman's investigation is free, thorough, and independent, this requirement is not unreasonable, and the courts have consistently given effect to it.

A complaint is "determined" for this purpose at the following points: when the Ombudsman has made a report and recommendation to the agency; when a veto (Order in Council) is entered that precludes the making of a recommendation; or when the Ombudsman informs you that the request was justifiably refused.

Once the Ombudsman has determined your complaint, the path to the courts opens. What happens next depends on the outcome of the Ombudsman process and whether a veto has been exercised.

Judicial Review of the Executive Override (Order in Council)

The most direct route to court arises when the Ombudsman has recommended that information be released, but the executive has overridden that recommendation by Order in Council (under the OIA) or by resolution of the local authority (under LGOIMA).

Section 32B of the OIA provides a statutory right of "review" in the High Court. Despite the use of the word "review," this is, strictly speaking, a statutory appeal. You can apply to the High Court on the ground that the Order in Council was "beyond the powers conferred by sections 32 and 32A or was otherwise wrong in law."

The grounds of review are therefore: that the Order in Council exceeded the powers given to the Governor-General in Council (for example, because it was made for reasons that were not before the Ombudsman, which is prohibited by section 32A); or that it was "otherwise wrong in law" (which includes errors of legal interpretation, procedural failures, and potentially unreasonableness in the public law sense).

This statutory review effectively displaces ordinary judicial review where a veto has been entered. There would be little point in a court entertaining an application for ordinary judicial review when a specific statutory review mechanism is available.

The solicitor-and-client costs rule

One of the most striking features of section 32B is its costs provision. Unless the High Court is satisfied that your application has not been reasonably or properly brought, the court must order that your costs on a solicitor-and-client basis be paid by the Crown (or, in the case of LGOIMA, by the local authority), regardless of the outcome of the application.

This is an extraordinary provision. In ordinary litigation, the losing party typically pays the winning party's costs. Under section 32B, even if you lose your application, the Crown pays your legal costs, provided the application was reasonably and properly brought. The provision was included in the 1987 amendments as part of the package that replaced the individual ministerial veto with the collective Cabinet veto. It ensures that the cost of litigation does not deter requesters from challenging an executive override of an Ombudsman recommendation.

The solicitor-and-client costs rule applies only to the statutory review of an Order in Council under section 32B. It does not apply to ordinary judicial review of agency decisions in other circumstances.

Appeals

Any party dissatisfied with the High Court's decision on a section 32B application can appeal to the Court of Appeal.

Judicial Review of Agency Decisions on Other Grounds

Outside the specific section 32B mechanism, the courts can also be involved in OIA matters through ordinary judicial review.

After the Ombudsman upholds the refusal

If you complain to the Ombudsman and the Ombudsman determines that the agency's refusal was justified, you can seek judicial review of the agency's original decision. In this scenario, you may also challenge the Ombudsman's determination itself, on the basis that the Ombudsman made an error of law.

However, you will bear the cost of these proceedings yourself. There is no solicitor-and-client costs indemnity for ordinary judicial review.

The leading case on this point is *Commissioner of Police v Ombudsman* (1985, High Court; 1988, Court of Appeal), in which the police sought judicial review of the Ombudsman's recommendation that police briefs of evidence be disclosed. The case established that the Ombudsman's recommendations are judicially reviewable, and it explored the scope and standard of review applicable to OIA decisions.

Judicial review of other decisions

Judicial review is also potentially available in relation to other decisions under the OIA, including decisions by agencies to give a section 10 notice (neither confirming nor denying the existence of information), and the exercise of the veto powers under section 31 by the Prime Minister or Attorney-General over the Ombudsman's investigation process.

Decisions under Parts 3 and 4

The section 34 restriction on judicial review applies only to decisions under Part 2 (requests for official information). It does not apply to Parts 3 and 4 (access to internal decision-making rules, statements of reasons for decisions, and personal information requests by corporate entities). These Parts confer legal rights of access, and those rights can be vindicated directly in the courts without first going to the Ombudsman.

The Danks Committee considered it inappropriate for the Ombudsman to make binding determinations of legal right, which is properly the role of the courts. This also explains why there is no veto power under Parts 3 and 4: since the Ombudsman can only recommend (not order) disclosure under these Parts, a veto was considered unnecessary.

In practice, however, the paradox noted by the Eagles/Taggart/Liddell text is that the legal right of access under Parts 3 and 4 is in some ways less effective than the mere entitlement to official information under Part 2. Under Part 2, the Ombudsman's recommendation becomes legally binding after 21 working days unless a veto is exercised, and the veto itself can be challenged in court at the Crown's expense. Under Parts 3 and 4, if an agency refuses to follow the Ombudsman's recommendation, the only remedy is for the requester to seek a court declaration or mandamus at their own expense. The cost of litigation will, in most cases, deter individual requesters from pursuing this path. The Eagles/Taggart/Liddell text argues that there is an "unassailable case" for a solicitor-and-client costs provision in Part 5 similar to that in section 32B, but this reform has not been enacted.

Practical Considerations: Cost, Time, and When Litigation Makes Sense

Going to court under the OIA is a serious step that most requesters will never need to take. Before considering litigation, think carefully about the following.

Cost

Unless you are challenging an Order in Council under section 32B (where the Crown pays your costs), you will bear your own legal costs. Judicial review proceedings in the High Court are expensive. Legal fees for a contested judicial review application can run into tens of thousands of dollars, and if you lose, you may be ordered to pay the agency's costs as well. Legal aid is theoretically available for judicial review proceedings, but the eligibility criteria are strict.

The cost barrier is the single greatest obstacle to court involvement in OIA disputes. It means that, in practice, only well-funded organisations, interest groups, or individuals with strong financial backing can afford to litigate. The Ombudsman process, which is free, will always be the preferred first option.

Time

Court proceedings are slow. An application for judicial review will typically take months to prepare, file, and argue. The court will need time to consider the matter and deliver its judgment. If there is an appeal, the process can take years. For requesters who need information quickly, litigation is not a practical remedy.

When litigation makes sense

Despite the obstacles, there are situations where going to court may be the right choice.

Challenging an Order in Council. If the executive has vetoed an Ombudsman recommendation, section 32B provides a purpose-built mechanism for challenging that decision, with costs protection. Given the rarity of the veto, this scenario is unlikely to arise, but if it does, the costs provision makes litigation viable.

Establishing a legal principle. If your case raises a novel or important question of law about the interpretation of the OIA, a court decision may have lasting value beyond your individual dispute. Interest groups, media organisations, and public interest litigators may be willing to fund or support litigation that tests the boundaries of the Act.

Vindicating a right under Parts 3 or 4. If you have a legal right of access to internal decision-making rules (section 22), reasons for a decision (section 23), or personal information as a corporate entity (Part 4), and the agency refuses to comply with the Ombudsman's recommendation, court proceedings to enforce your right may be the only remaining option. The absence of a costs provision makes this expensive, but the existence of a clear legal right may make it a stronger case for legal aid or pro bono representation.

Where the Ombudsman's determination is wrong in law. If you believe the Ombudsman has made an error of law in determining your complaint, judicial review of the Ombudsman's determination is available. This is a narrow ground, because the courts will generally accord significant respect to the Ombudsman's expertise in OIA matters, but it is available in principle.

Where an agency refuses to comply with a binding recommendation. If the Ombudsman recommends release, the public duty to comply arises after 21 working days, and the agency does not exercise the formal override, but simply refuses to comply, the matter can be referred to the Solicitor-General for enforcement proceedings. In the few cases where this has occurred (all in the 1990s, involving organisations outside the core state sector), the agencies complied before the matter reached court. But the enforcement mechanism exists.

Alternatives to full litigation

Before committing to full court proceedings, consider whether there are intermediate steps that might achieve your objective. A letter from a lawyer citing the relevant provisions and signalling an intention to seek judicial review can sometimes prompt an agency to reconsider its position. Involvement of the Ombudsman in a second round of investigation (if circumstances have changed) may also be productive. And in some cases, political pressure through media coverage, parliamentary questions, or public advocacy may achieve what litigation cannot.

The courts are an important part of the OIA system, but they are the remedy of last resort. For most requesters, most of the time, the Ombudsman is the right place to be. The courts stand behind the Ombudsman process, providing a backstop of legal enforceability that gives the system its ultimate credibility, even if that backstop is rarely invoked.

PART FIVE

WHEN THINGS GO WRONG

CHAPTER 16

Common Problems and How to Handle Them

The previous chapters have explained the legal framework: your rights, the agency's obligations, the grounds for refusal, and the complaint process. This chapter is different. It deals with the messy reality of what actually goes wrong, and what you can do about it.

Every experienced requester has encountered the problems described here. Some are the result of genuine administrative difficulty. Others reflect a culture within parts of government that still treats the release of information as a risk to be managed rather than a right to be honoured. The key to handling these problems effectively is understanding the difference, and knowing your options in each case.

Delays and Non-Responses

Delay is the single most common complaint about the OIA system. Research into the Act's administration has consistently found that it is the issue that generates the strongest feelings among requesters. Many assume that delay is a deliberate tactic to manage the political value of information, and while that is not always the case, the perception is widespread and not without foundation.

If an agency has not responded to your request within 20 working days (or within an extended timeframe, if one has been validly notified), you have several options.

Start by sending a polite follow-up email to the person or team that received your request. Note the date you made the request, note that the statutory time limit has passed, and ask when you can expect a response. Keep the tone constructive. Many delays are caused by internal bottlenecks (senior sign-off, ministerial notification, third-party consultation) rather than bad faith, and a reminder will often move things along.

If you do not receive a substantive response within a few working days, send a more formal follow-up. This time, note explicitly that the agency is in breach of its obligations under section 15 of the OIA (or section 13 of LGOIMA), which requires a decision to be made and communicated as soon as reasonably practicable and no later than 20 working days after the request is received. State that you intend to complain to the Ombudsman if you do not receive a response by a specific date. Give the agency a reasonable period, but do not wait indefinitely.

If the agency still does not respond, complain to the Ombudsman. You do not need to wait for a formal refusal. The Ombudsman has jurisdiction to investigate delays, and does so regularly. In your complaint, include your original request, any correspondence with the agency, and the dates involved.

Throughout this process, keep records of everything. Note the date of your original request, the date of each follow-up, and the date of any response. If conversations happen by phone, follow up with an email confirming what was discussed. These records will be essential if you complain to the Ombudsman.

The "Deemed Refusal"

When an agency fails to respond to your request within the statutory time limit, the law treats this as a refusal. This is sometimes called a "deemed refusal." The practical significance is that once the time limit has passed without a response, you have the same right to complain to the Ombudsman as you would if the agency had sent you a letter refusing your request outright.

The deemed refusal concept exists because the OIA would be meaningless if agencies could avoid accountability simply by not responding. The Ombudsman has confirmed that a failure to respond within the statutory time limit gives rise to a right of complaint, regardless of whether the agency intended to refuse or was simply running behind.

One important point: a deemed refusal does not mean the agency has no obligation to respond. Even after the time limit has passed, the agency remains obligated to make a decision and communicate it to you. The deemed refusal simply gives you the right to seek the Ombudsman's intervention while you wait.

Extensions That Seem Unreasonable or Are Made Too Late

The OIA allows agencies to extend the 20-working-day time limit, but only on specific grounds: either because consultations necessary to make a decision cannot reasonably be completed in time, or because the request involves a large quantity of information and responding within the original timeframe would unreasonably interfere with the agency's operations. The extension must be for a "reasonable period" having regard to the circumstances, and the agency must notify you of the extension, the reason for it, and your right to complain to the Ombudsman.

Three problems commonly arise with extensions.

First, agencies sometimes extend for reasons that do not fall within the statutory grounds. Being busy with other work, or having staff on leave, is not a valid basis for extension. The grounds are specific: large volume or necessary consultations. If an agency cites a reason that does not fit either of these categories, you can challenge the extension.

Second, agencies sometimes extend for periods that seem unreasonably long. An extension of several months for a straightforward request involving modest consultation is unlikely to be reasonable. The Ombudsman has found that extensions must be proportionate to the actual difficulty involved. If you receive an extension that seems disproportionate, ask the agency to explain why that period is necessary, and if you are not satisfied, complain.

Third, and most importantly, agencies sometimes notify an extension after the original 20 working days have already passed. The law is clear: the extension must be notified within the original time limit. An extension notified after day 20 is invalid. If you receive a late extension notice, write to the agency pointing out that the notice was given outside the statutory timeframe and that you consider the agency to be in breach of its obligations. Then complain to the Ombudsman.

Being Told the Information Is "Not Held"

One of the most frustrating experiences for a requester is being told that the information you asked for is not held by the agency, when you have good reason to believe it exists. There are several reasons this happens, and understanding them will help you respond effectively.

Sometimes the information genuinely does not exist in the form you assumed. You may have asked for a report that was never written, or for data that was never compiled in the way you expected. In these cases, the agency's response is technically correct, but it may still be unhelpful. The Ombudsman's guidance makes clear that if an agency holds information that is relevant to your request but in a different form than the one you specified, it should tell you what it does hold and offer to provide that instead.

Sometimes the information exists but the agency cannot find it. The OIA distinguishes between documents that do not exist and documents that cannot be found despite reasonable efforts. Before relying on section 18(e), an agency must make a reasonable search. This means asking relevant staff to look, searching electronic systems using appropriate terms, consulting information management staff, and following up on obvious leads. The search must be thorough and intelligent, not perfunctory. If you suspect the agency's search was inadequate, ask what searches were conducted, who was asked, what systems were checked, and what search terms were used. You are entitled to this information, and it will form the basis of any complaint.

Sometimes the information should exist but was not properly created or retained. The Ombudsman has found that agencies cannot rely on their own administrative failures to justify a "not held" response. In one notable case, the Chief Ombudsman found that a government department should have held records of alleged staff assaults under its own operating manual, and that the difficulty in providing the information was the department's own fault for not keeping proper records. The department agreed to collate and release what it could find, and to change its practices going forward.

If you receive a "not held" response and you believe the information should exist, your options are: ask the agency to explain what searches it conducted and why it believes the information is not held; suggest specific places or systems the agency might look; ask whether the information might be held by another agency (which would trigger a transfer obligation); and, if you are not satisfied, complain to the Ombudsman, who has the power to review the adequacy of the agency's search.

Excessive Redactions

Agencies have the power under section 17 of the OIA to release documents with deletions where there is good reason to withhold some of the information they contain. This is the power of partial release, and it is an important feature of the Act: it means that the existence of some sensitive material within a document does not justify withholding the entire document.

The problem arises when partial release becomes so heavy-handed that the released information is meaningless. Pages of black ink with a few stray prepositions visible do not serve the purposes of the Act. If you receive a response that has been redacted to the point of uselessness, there are several things you can do.

First, check the reasons given for each withholding. Under section 17(2), the agency must tell you the reason for withholding the redacted information. If the response simply says "section 9(2)(g)(i)" next to a page of black, that is not adequate. You are entitled to understand why each category of information was withheld, and you can ask for the grounds in support of that reason.

Second, consider whether the redactions are consistent with the grounds cited. If the agency has cited privacy (section 9(2)(a)) as the reason, the redactions should be limited to information that identifies or could identify a natural person. If entire paragraphs of policy analysis have been redacted under a privacy ground, something has gone wrong. Similarly, if free and frank opinions (section 9(2)(g)(i)) has been cited, factual and background material should not have been caught by the redaction.

Third, look at whether the agency has applied the public interest test. For any withholding under section 9, the agency must consider whether the public interest in release outweighs the need to withhold. If the response makes no mention of the public interest test, or applies it in a formulaic way without genuine analysis, that is a ground for complaint.

Fourth, complain to the Ombudsman. The Ombudsman has the power to review the withheld information and form an independent view on whether each redaction was justified. In many cases, the Ombudsman's investigation results in the release of additional material that the agency had redacted. Excessive redaction is one of the most common issues the Ombudsman deals with, and one where the complaint process is most likely to produce results.

Being Asked to Narrow Your Request

Agencies are entitled to consult you about the scope of your request, and in many cases this is a constructive process. If your request captures thousands of documents and would take weeks to process, a conversation about what you actually need can benefit everyone. The Act explicitly contemplates this kind of dialogue, and the Ombudsman encourages it.

The difficulty arises when the request to narrow is not genuinely collaborative but is instead a strategy to reduce the scope of the response to the point where nothing useful is released. Some requesters have described receiving suggestions to narrow that would effectively gut their request, or being told that the agency will refuse under section 18(f) (substantial collation or research) unless they agree to accept a small fraction of what they asked for.

The key to handling this well is to engage constructively without surrendering the substance of what you need. Here are some practical approaches.

Respond to the agency's concerns and ask for specifics. If the agency says your request is too broad, ask exactly how many documents are in scope, how much time would be involved, and which parts of the request are causing the most difficulty. This information will help you make informed decisions about what to prioritise.

Be willing to adjust the scope where you can do so without losing what matters. Narrowing a date range, excluding categories of documents you do not actually need (such as duplicate copies, routine administrative emails, or documents already publicly available), or agreeing to receive information in a summary or alternative format can reduce the agency's workload significantly while preserving the substance of your request.

If the agency proposes a narrowing that would effectively gut your request, say so. Explain what you need and why. Propose alternatives of your own. Ask whether the agency could meet the request if it charged you, or if it extended the time limit. Both of these options must be considered before a refusal under section 18(f), and if the agency has not genuinely considered them, its refusal is vulnerable to challenge.

Keep a written record of the consultation. If the conversation happens by phone, follow up with an email confirming what was discussed and what was agreed. This protects you if there is a later dispute about what you consented to.

If the agency ultimately refuses your request after consultation, remember that the refusal is reviewable by the Ombudsman. The Ombudsman will look at whether the agency genuinely considered all the alternatives before refusing, whether the consultation was conducted in good faith, and whether the refusal was proportionate to the actual difficulty involved.

Agencies That Try to Discourage You

Most agencies process OIA requests professionally and in good faith. But some requesters encounter informal resistance: phone calls suggesting that you withdraw your request, comments about the request being a waste of the agency's time, warnings that you will be charged a large amount, or suggestions that you should find the information through other channels.

This kind of pushback is not sanctioned by the Act and is not acceptable. The OIA gives you the right to request any official information, and the agency's obligation is to process the request in accordance with the law. The agency may consult you about scope, may charge you for the supply of information, or may extend the time limit where the statutory grounds are met. It may not pressure you to withdraw.

If you encounter informal discouragement, the best response is to stay calm, stay polite, and stay firm. If the conversation happens by phone, follow up with an email confirming what was said and reaffirming your request. If the agency raises concerns about scope or workload, engage with those concerns constructively (as discussed above), but do not agree to withdraw unless you genuinely no longer need the information.

If the behaviour is persistent or particularly egregious, you can raise it with the Ombudsman. While the Ombudsman's primary jurisdiction is over specific decisions (refusals, delays, charges), the Ombudsman also has a broader role in promoting good OIA practice and can address systemic issues with individual agencies.

Being Told to Use a Different Process

Agencies sometimes respond to OIA requests by telling the requester that the information should be sought through a different process: the Privacy Act for personal information, the discovery process in litigation, parliamentary questions for politically sensitive material, or a direct approach to a particular official or team.

In some cases, this advice is correct and helpful. If you are seeking your own personal information, the Privacy Act does provide a more appropriate (and in some respects stronger) right of access. If you are a party to litigation and the information is relevant to your case, discovery may be a more effective route. The agency is entitled to point this out.

But in other cases, the suggestion to use a different process is a way of deflecting the request rather than dealing with it. The OIA applies to all official information, regardless of whether other processes might also provide access to some of it. The existence of an alternative remedy does not remove the requester's right to use the OIA. The Ombudsman has confirmed this repeatedly.

If you are told to use a different process, consider whether the advice is genuinely in your interest. If the Privacy Act would give you faster or more complete access to your personal information, it may be worth following that path. But if you are seeking information that goes beyond your personal details (for example, an agency's policy on a matter that affected you, or correspondence between officials about your case), the OIA is the appropriate route and you should not be deflected.

If the agency refuses your OIA request on the basis that you should use a different process, check whether the statutory grounds support that refusal. There is no general ground in section 18 for refusing a request because an alternative process exists. The agency would need to point to a specific provision, such as section 18(c)(i) (disclosure would be contrary to another enactment), or a specific withholding ground under section 9. If the refusal does not cite a valid ground, it is challengeable.

Agencies Using Charges as a Deterrent

The power to charge for the supply of official information is legitimate and necessary for genuinely large requests. But research into the OIA's administration has found widespread perception among requesters that charging is sometimes used as a tool to discourage requests rather than to genuinely manage costs.

The signs of deterrent charging include: a charge estimate that seems disproportionate to the scope of the request; a charge that includes activities that cannot lawfully be charged for (such as decision-making time, general overheads, or the cost of obtaining legal advice on what to release); a charge imposed on a request that seems straightforward; or a sudden charge notification on a type of request that the same agency has previously handled without charge.

If you suspect that a charge is being used as a deterrent, there are several steps you can take.

Ask for a detailed breakdown of how the charge was calculated. You are entitled to this. The breakdown should identify the specific activities, the time estimated for each, and the rate applied. Compare this against the Government's Charging Guidelines, which specify what can and cannot be charged for, and what rates are appropriate. The first half-hour of search and retrieval time should not be charged. Decision-making time cannot be charged. The hourly rate should reflect the actual cost of the staff member doing the work, not senior management or legal counsel rates.

Consider whether you can reduce the charge by narrowing your request or accepting information in a different format (for example, inspecting documents rather than receiving copies, or accepting electronic copies rather than hard copies).

If you believe the charge is unreasonable, say so. Ask the agency to reconsider, and explain why. Point to the Government's Charging Guidelines. If the request serves a genuine public interest (for example, if you are a journalist investigating a matter of public concern, or a community group seeking information about a decision that affects your community), ask for remission of the charge on public interest grounds. If payment would cause you financial hardship, explain this and ask for remission on hardship grounds.

If the agency will not budge, complain to the Ombudsman. Charges are reviewable, and the Ombudsman has a track record of finding that charges were unreasonable or improperly calculated. In one well-known case, the Ombudsman found that an agency could not withdraw an offer to release information on payment of a charge after the requester had accepted the charge and paid the deposit. The agency was required to honour its original offer.

Repeat Requests and the Risk of Being Labelled "Vexatious"

If you use the OIA regularly, particularly if you make frequent requests to the same agency, you may encounter the suggestion that your requests are vexatious. Section 18(h) of the OIA allows agencies to refuse requests that are frivolous or vexatious, or where the information sought is trivial. But the threshold for invoking this ground is high, and the Ombudsman has consistently emphasised that it should not be used to punish frequent requesters or to avoid dealing with inconvenient requests.

Making a large number of requests, by itself, does not make any individual request vexatious. The question is always about the nature of the specific request, assessed in light of the surrounding circumstances. The Ombudsman looks at whether the request amounts to an abuse of the right to access information, rather than a legitimate exercise of that right. Factors that may indicate abuse include: requests made solely to harass or annoy staff; requests that are part of a campaign of conduct designed to disrupt the agency's operations; requests for information that the requester already has and does not need again; and requests framed in language that is aggressive, offensive, or threatening.

Factors that weigh against a finding of vexatiousness include: the requester has a legitimate interest in the information; the requester's grievance is to some extent justified; the agency's own handling of earlier requests has contributed to the current difficulties; and the information has genuine value to the requester or the public.

The Ombudsman has also noted that a repeat request for information on the same subject is not the same as a repeat request for the same information. If new information has been created or received since your last request, a new request on the same topic captures different material and is not a "repeat" in any meaningful sense. Similarly, a request for the same information in a different format (for example, in electronic form after receiving it on paper) is a new request and should be treated on its merits.

If an agency labels your request as vexatious and you believe this is wrong, you should complain to the Ombudsman. In your complaint, explain the legitimate purpose behind your request, note any history of the agency's own failings in handling your earlier requests, and point out that frequency alone does not equal vexatiousness. The Ombudsman will assess the matter independently.

To reduce the risk of being labelled vexatious in the first place, there are several practical steps you can take. Keep your requests focused and clearly worded. Avoid language that could be interpreted as aggressive or personal, even if you are frustrated. If you are making follow-up requests because earlier responses were inadequate, explain this calmly and specifically. Do not make requests for information you already have unless you have a good reason for needing it again (such as needing it in a different format). If the agency contacts you to discuss your requests, engage with them. The Ombudsman has noted that agencies should try to talk to requesters before resorting to section 18(h), and a requester who refuses to engage may weaken their position.

Practical Advice for All of These Situations

Several principles apply across all of the common problems described in this chapter.

First, always respond in writing. Even if the agency contacts you by phone, follow up with an email confirming the conversation. Written records are essential for any complaint to the Ombudsman, and they discipline both sides to be clear and accurate about what has been communicated.

Second, engage constructively before escalating. Many problems can be resolved through direct communication with the agency. A polite, informed follow-up that demonstrates your understanding of the Act and its requirements will often produce a better result than an immediate complaint.

Third, know when to escalate. If direct engagement does not resolve the problem within a reasonable period, do not hesitate to complain to the Ombudsman. The complaint process is free, it is your right, and it exists precisely for these situations. The Ombudsman's preliminary enquiries alone resolve many complaints without the need for a formal investigation, simply because the fact of an Ombudsman enquiry focuses the agency's attention.

Fourth, be persistent but proportionate. The OIA is a powerful tool, but it works best when requesters use it thoughtfully. Prioritise the requests that matter most to you. Be willing to make reasonable compromises on scope or format. But do not abandon a legitimate request simply because the agency makes it difficult. The principle of availability exists for a reason, and every requester who successfully asserts their rights contributes to a stronger culture of openness in New Zealand's public institutions.

PART SIX

ADVANCED TOPICS

CHAPTER 17

Requesting from Ministers

Making an OIA request to a Minister of the Crown is legally straightforward but practically complex. Ministers are subject to the OIA in their own right, separately from the departments they oversee. In theory, the same rules apply: the Minister must make a decision as soon as reasonably practicable and no later than 20 working days, must give reasons for any refusal, and is subject to the Ombudsman's review jurisdiction. In practice, however, the dynamics of requesting from Ministers are different in ways that every experienced requester needs to understand.

This chapter explains how Ministerial OIA requests differ from departmental ones, how the transfer and consultation mechanisms work, what the "no surprises" convention means for your request, how Ministerial offices actually handle the process, and what political considerations you should be aware of. It also offers practical guidance on navigating the boundary between Ministers and departments, which is one of the most contested and least well-understood aspects of the OIA.

How Ministerial OIA Requests Differ from Departmental Ones

When you make a request to a government department, you are dealing with a bureaucratic organisation that (usually) has a dedicated OIA team, established processes for logging and tracking requests, and staff whose job it is to search for information and prepare responses. The decision is typically made by a senior official, and while there may be consultation with the Minister's office before the response is sent, the legal responsibility for the decision remains with the department.

When you make a request directly to a Minister, the dynamics change. The Minister's office is a small, politically staffed operation. It typically consists of the Minister, a private secretary, a press secretary, one or more political advisers, and a small number of administrative staff. It does not have the same systems, resources, or institutional knowledge as a department. In practice, the Minister's office will often ask the relevant department to assist with searching for information and preparing a draft response, but the decision remains the Minister's.

The information that a Minister holds in their official capacity is also different from what a department holds. Ministers hold Cabinet papers (which they "own" even though departments draft them), correspondence with other Ministers, briefings from their departments, records of decisions they have made in the exercise of statutory functions, and communications with stakeholders in their Ministerial capacity. They also hold information that relates to their political role: communications with coalition partners, political advisers' briefings on media strategy, and material relating to parliamentary debates.

Crucially, the OIA only applies to information held by a Minister in their official capacity. Information held in a Minister's capacity as a member of a political party, as an electorate MP, or in a purely personal capacity is not "official information" and is not subject to the Act. This distinction can be difficult to draw in practice. Research into the OIA's administration has documented cases where the line between a Minister's official and political roles was genuinely blurred. If you are requesting information from a Minister and the response claims that the information is not held in an official capacity, you should consider whether that claim is sustainable given the nature of the information and the context in which it was generated or received.

The Transfer, Consultation, and Notification Framework

The OIA creates a framework of three mechanisms for managing the relationship between departments and Ministers when an OIA request is received. Understanding these mechanisms is essential for requesters, because they determine who makes the decision on your request, how long the process takes, and what kind of political input is involved.

Transfer is the mechanism by which responsibility for deciding on a request is formally shifted from a department to a Minister (or vice versa).

Under section 14 of the OIA, an agency must transfer a request if the information is believed to be held by another agency, or is believed to be more closely connected with the functions of another agency. A Minister is an "agency" for this purpose.

The key question for transfer is whether the information is "more closely connected with the Minister's functions." The Ombudsman's guidance identifies the functions of Ministers by reference to the Cabinet Manual: Ministers take significant decisions and determine government policy through the Cabinet process; they exercise statutory functions under legislation within their portfolios; they determine the policy direction and priorities for their departments; and they have a political role in maintaining government stability. In contrast, officials are responsible for implementing policy, providing day-to-day operational management, and supporting Ministers in carrying out their Ministerial functions.

When a transfer occurs, several things happen. The department sends the request (and, crucially, the relevant information) to the Minister's office. The 20 working day clock restarts from the day after the transfer is received by the Minister. The requester must be notified of the transfer. From the requester's perspective, transfer adds delay: up to 10 working days for the transfer itself, then up to 20 working days for the Minister to respond. In practice, the delay is often longer than this.

Transfer must be based on a genuine and reasonable belief that the information is more closely connected with the Minister's functions. The Ombudsman has found that blanket policies of transferring all requests from a particular source (such as all media requests) or all requests on a particular subject are unlawful. Each request must be assessed individually on the basis of the specific information at issue.

Consultation is the mechanism by which a department seeks the Minister's comments before making its own decision on a request. Unlike transfer, consultation does not shift responsibility for the decision. The department remains the decision-maker. It is simply seeking the Minister's input, which it must consider in good faith and with an open mind before deciding what to do.

The Ombudsman has made clear that consultation is not negotiation and does not require agreement. The department must consider the Minister's views but is not bound by them. If there is a disagreement between the department and the Minister about whether to release information, the department retains the legal authority to make the decision. In practice, however, research into the OIA's administration has found that departments often find it difficult to release information when the Minister's office objects. One public servant described the dynamic this way: the department might be relaxed about release but the Minister sees a reason to withhold, and managing that interface becomes the central challenge.

The Ombudsman has also found that a blanket policy of consulting the Minister on all OIA requests is unlawful. In one notable case, a department was found to have adopted a practice of forwarding all OIA responses to the Minister for "information and clearance." The Ombudsman wrote to the Minister to explain that this practice was not contemplated by the OIA and that seeking ministerial clearance or approval of agency OIA responses is an abdication of the agency's responsibilities and would breach section 15(4) of the Act, which requires departments to act independently.

Notification is the lightest-touch mechanism. It simply means telling the Minister about the decision the department has made, after that decision has been taken, so that the Minister can prepare for the possibility of public or political commentary. Notification gives the Minister no input into the decision. It is not provided for in the OIA itself but has evolved out of the "no surprises" principle in the Cabinet Manual, which requires agencies to inform Ministers promptly of matters of significance that may become the subject of public debate.

The important point for requesters is that notification, properly conducted, should not add delay. The decision has already been made. The information is being provided to the Minister for their awareness, not for their approval. If an agency delays communicating a decision to the requester while it notifies the Minister, this may constitute "undue delay" in the release of information, which is reviewable by the Ombudsman.

The "No Surprises" Convention and How It Affects Processing

The "no surprises" convention is not a legal requirement under the OIA. It is a constitutional convention, derived from paragraph 3.26(a) of the Cabinet Manual, which states that agencies should inform Ministers promptly of matters of significance within their portfolio responsibilities, particularly where these may be controversial or become the subject of public debate.

In the context of OIA requests, the "no surprises" convention has become the primary justification for Ministerial involvement in departmental OIA processing. Its practical effect is significant: departments routinely notify Ministers of upcoming OIA responses, and in many cases consult them before making a decision. This adds time to the process and introduces a layer of political consideration that the Act's framers may not have anticipated.

The Ombudsman has acknowledged that the "no surprises" principle has a legitimate role in the OIA process, but has drawn firm boundaries around it. Notification is permissible provided it does not interfere with the agency's ability to comply with its statutory obligations: to make the decision itself, free from improper influence; to communicate the decision within the statutory time limit; and to release information without undue delay. Consultation is permissible where the agency genuinely needs the Minister's input to make a fully informed decision. Neither is permissible as a mechanism for giving the Minister a veto over the release of information.

For requesters, the practical implication is that the "no surprises" convention often adds several days to the processing of any request that touches on politically sensitive matters. This is one reason why many departments use the full 20 working days even for requests that could be answered more quickly. If you suspect that delay in your request is caused by the notification or consultation process running beyond what is reasonable, you can raise this with the Ombudsman, who has jurisdiction to investigate delays and has commented critically on cases where ministerial processes have contributed to late responses.

Ministerial Offices and the Handling of OIA Requests in Practice

The practical reality of how OIA requests are handled within Ministerial offices is something that the legislation does not describe but that research into the Act's administration has documented in considerable detail.

When a department receives a request that may involve the Minister's interests, the typical process is as follows. The OIA team identifies the request as one that may require transfer, consultation, or notification. The team prepares a draft response (or, in transfer cases, a recommendation about transfer). The draft is reviewed internally, often by legal advisers and senior officials. It is then sent to the Minister's office, either for decision (if transferred), for comment (if consultation), or for information (if notification). The Minister's office reviews the material, often through the political advisers or press secretary rather than the Minister personally.

Comments or a decision come back to the department, and the response is finalised and sent to the requester.

The role of political advisers in this process is a source of significant tension. Research has found that political advisers, whose primary task is managing the Minister's media and political profile, tend to be among the most conservative voices on release questions. Several public servants interviewed for research into the OIA's operation described pressure from political advisers to find grounds to withhold information, even where the department's own assessment was that release was appropriate. One described the dynamic as political advisers having a deeply sceptical view of the public service and distrusting not only requesters and the Ombudsman but also the officials advising them.

The accountability gap is also significant. Public servants are accountable through the Ombudsman for their OIA decisions. Ministers are accountable through Parliament. But political advisers sit in between, exercising significant influence over OIA outcomes without being directly accountable to either mechanism. This is a structural feature of the system that requesters should be aware of, even though there is little they can do about it directly.

For requesters, the practical consequence of all this is that requests involving politically sensitive information, or requests from journalists or political parties, are likely to receive closer scrutiny, take longer to process, and result in more conservative withholding decisions than requests that do not engage the Minister's political interests. This is not necessarily improper (Ministers do have legitimate interests in knowing what information is about to enter the public domain), but it can and does shade into delay and over-withholding in some cases.

Political Considerations: Elections, Announcements, and Media Management

The OIA operates in a political environment, and requesters need to be realistic about the ways in which political considerations can affect the handling of their requests. This does not mean accepting political interference as legitimate, but it does mean being aware of the patterns and knowing how to respond.

Election periods are a particular flashpoint. Research has found that OIA processing is affected by the election cycle: requests that touch on policy commitments, government performance, or politically contentious issues are handled with particular care (and sometimes particular slowness) in the months before an election. The legal position is clear: the OIA applies with equal force during election periods, and neither the imminence of an election nor the political sensitivity of the information is a ground for withholding or delay. But the practical reality is that Ministerial offices become more cautious, and the "no surprises" convention is applied more conservatively, when the political stakes are highest.

Policy announcements can also affect OIA timing. If a requester asks for information about a policy that the government is planning to announce, the agency may invoke section 18(d) (information soon to be publicly available) to defer release until after the announcement. This ground is legitimate in principle, but agencies sometimes stretch it by claiming that information will be "soon" publicly available when no firm date for release has been set. If you receive a section 18(d) refusal, ask when the information will be available and follow up if the promised date passes without publication.

Media management is a more subtle and pervasive concern. Some agencies time the release of OIA responses to minimise media impact, for example by releasing on Friday afternoons or at times when the news cycle has moved on. Some release information to others (including friendly media outlets) before providing it to the requester. The Ombudsman has found that releasing information to others before the requester can constitute undue delay. Some agencies structure their responses to present the released information in the most favourable light, for example by attaching contextual briefings or press releases.

None of these practices is necessarily unlawful, but they can undermine the purposes of the Act. If you suspect that an OIA response has been timed or structured for political rather than administrative reasons, the best response is usually to note it and move on. If the timing has resulted in a breach of the statutory time limit, you can complain to the Ombudsman. If information has been released to others before you received it, that too is a matter the Ombudsman can investigate.

The Difficulty of the Minister/Department Boundary and How to Navigate It

The boundary between Ministers and departments is one of the most contested and practically difficult aspects of the OIA. The Act treats them as separate decision-makers with separate obligations, but in reality they are deeply intertwined. A Minister's policy priorities drive the department's work. The department's analysis and advice inform the Minister's decisions. Cabinet papers are drafted by officials but owned by Ministers. Correspondence with stakeholders may be signed by the Minister but prepared by departmental staff. In many cases, both the department and the Minister will hold relevant information, and the question of who should decide on the request is genuinely difficult.

Research into the OIA has identified this boundary as one of the biggest structural problems with the Act. The transfer provisions were designed for a simpler model of the relationship between Ministers and departments, and they do not always fit comfortably with the modern reality of highly politicised accountability frameworks, coalition government, and the expanding role of Ministerial offices. Several commentators have observed that the provisions need to be stretched and contorted to fit with reality.

For requesters, this creates several practical challenges.

Choosing where to send your request. As a general rule, if you want operational information, departmental analysis, policy advice, or administrative records, direct your request to the department. If you want information about the Minister's decision-making, communications with other Ministers, or material that is genuinely Ministerial in character (such as the Minister's comments on a Cabinet paper, or correspondence between Ministers about a policy issue), consider directing your request to the Minister. If in doubt, direct it to the department. The department has better systems for processing requests and can transfer to the Minister if necessary.

Dealing with transfers. If the department transfers your request to the Minister, be aware that this adds delay (the clock restarts) and shifts decision-making to a smaller, more politically oriented office. Ask the department to confirm that it has transferred the relevant information along with the request, so that the Minister has everything needed to make a decision. If you believe the transfer is inappropriate (for example, because the information is clearly operational and not closely connected with the Minister's functions), you can complain to the Ombudsman.

Avoiding the gap between departments and Ministers. One of the risks of the transfer system is that information falls into a gap: the department says the information is more closely connected with the Minister's functions, and the Minister's office says it does not hold the information (or that it is not held in the Minister's official capacity). If this happens, push back. Ask the department to explain its reasoning for the transfer. Ask the Minister's office to explain what searches it has conducted. If necessary, make parallel requests to both the department and the Minister to ensure that nothing is missed.

Dealing with consultation-related delays. If you suspect that your request to a department is being delayed because of consultation with the Minister's office, you have limited visibility into what is happening but several options available to you. If the department has not communicated a decision within 20 working days (or any extended period), complain to the Ombudsman about the delay. If the department extends the time limit on the grounds that consultations necessary to make a decision cannot be completed in time, consider whether the extension is reasonable. An extension to enable genuine consultation about the substance of the information (for example, whether a Cabinet paper can be released in full or needs some redaction) is more likely to be reasonable than an extension to enable the Minister's office to manage the political optics of the release.

Understanding what "official capacity" means for Ministers. If a Minister's office responds that the information is not held in the Minister's official capacity, scrutinise this claim carefully. The Ombudsman has found that the following factors are relevant: the nature and content of the information, the context in which it came to be held, and the use to which it has been put. Information that was generated in the course of the Minister's portfolio work, or that was used to inform Ministerial decisions, is likely to be held in an official capacity even if it also has a political dimension. The mere fact that information is politically sensitive does not take it outside the OIA.

Practical Advice for Requesters Dealing with Ministers

Several pieces of practical advice emerge from the material discussed in this chapter.

First, direct your request to the department whenever possible. Departments have better systems, more staff, and established processes for handling OIA requests. They are also more likely to respond within the statutory time limit. If the information is more closely connected with the Minister's functions, the department will transfer the request, but this at least ensures that the question of who should decide is addressed explicitly rather than by default.

Second, be specific about what you want. Ministerial offices are small and do not have the search capability of a department. A clearly worded request that identifies the information by topic, date range, and document type will be processed more efficiently than a broad request.

Third, be aware of timing. If you are requesting information that is politically sensitive, consider whether the timing of your request might affect how it is handled. Requests made close to elections, policy announcements, or parliamentary debates may receive more scrutiny and take longer to process. This is not a reason to delay your request, but it is a reason to build extra time into your planning.

Fourth, if you encounter delay, act quickly. Send a follow-up as soon as the time limit passes. Note that the "no surprises" convention does not override the statutory time limits. If you suspect that delay is caused by political considerations rather than genuine administrative difficulty, say so in your complaint to the Ombudsman. The Ombudsman has been clear that ministerial notification processes are not a legitimate reason for breaching the statutory time limit.

Fifth, keep records of all interactions. If the department tells you it has transferred your request to the Minister, note the date and ask for written confirmation. If the Minister's office contacts you by phone, follow up with an email confirming the conversation. Written records are your best protection if you need to complain to the Ombudsman about how your request has been handled.

The relationship between Ministers and departments under the OIA is, as one researcher described it, an area of considerable uncertainty about what is and is not appropriate, and the most obvious area where suspicion and distrust are growing. The Ombudsman's guidance provides a clear framework for how the relationship should work in principle. The practical reality is messier. But the framework gives requesters concrete standards against which to measure the treatment of their requests, and the Ombudsman provides an independent mechanism for enforcing those standards when they are not met.

CHAPTER 18

Requesting from Local Government under LGOIMA

The Local Government Official Information and Meetings Act 1987, commonly known as LGOIMA, extends the principles of the OIA to local government. It was modelled on the OIA and described by the courts as legislation of constitutional significance. In most respects, the two Acts operate in the same way: the principle of availability applies, the withholding grounds are tested in the same manner, the Ombudsman has the same review jurisdiction, and the practical process of making and responding to requests follows the same pattern.

But LGOIMA is not simply the OIA applied to councils. It has its own distinctive features, its own gaps, and its own practical challenges. This chapter explains the key differences between the OIA and LGOIMA, covers the additional LGOIMA provisions relating to meetings and agendas, describes the common types of local government information that requesters seek, and addresses the challenges specific to requesting from smaller, elected-member-governed local authorities.

Key Differences Between the OIA and LGOIMA

The LGOIMA mirrors the OIA in structure and substance, but with several important modifications. Understanding these differences is essential for anyone requesting information from local government.

Broader eligibility. Under the OIA, only New Zealand citizens, permanent residents, persons present in New Zealand, and bodies corporate incorporated in New Zealand may make requests. Under LGOIMA, there are no eligibility restrictions at all. Any person, anywhere in the world, may request official information from a local authority. This is a significant liberalisation. It means that overseas property owners, international researchers, foreign media, and anyone else with an interest in a New Zealand council's activities can make LGOIMA requests without having to establish any connection to New Zealand. This relaxation has caused no reported problems since the Act was passed.

Fewer withholding grounds. The LGOIMA has fewer grounds for withholding than the OIA. Several of the OIA's withholding grounds relate to matters that are relevant only to central government and have no equivalent in LGOIMA. Specifically, LGOIMA does not include grounds for withholding to protect national security, defence, or international relations (OIA section 6(a) and (b)); to prevent serious damage to the economy through premature disclosure of economic or financial policy decisions (OIA section 6(e)); to protect the substantial economic interests of New Zealand (OIA section 9(2)(d)); or to maintain constitutional conventions such as collective and individual ministerial responsibility and political neutrality of officials (OIA section 9(2)(f)). The absence of these grounds means that the range of interests that a local authority can invoke to justify withholding is narrower than the range available to central government agencies. In practice, the withholding grounds that local authorities use most frequently are the same as those used most frequently under the OIA: privacy (section 7(2)(a)), commercial sensitivity (section 7(2)(b)), confidentiality (section 7(2)(c)), free and frank opinions (section 7(2)(f)(i)), legal professional privilege (section 7(2)(g)), and negotiations (section 7(2)(i)).

Decision-making by the principal administrative officer. Under the OIA, there is no statutory specification of who within a department must make the decision on a request. Under LGOIMA, all decisions on requests are to be made by the "principal administrative officer" (typically the chief executive) or an authorised subordinate. This provision serves two purposes. It removes elected members from first-instance decision-making on requests, which would be problematic given the political dynamics of local government. And it avoids the practical difficulty that a council which meets only once a month would otherwise need to be formally convened to decide on requests within the 20 working day time limit.

The executive override mechanism. Under the OIA, if the Ombudsman recommends disclosure and the agency disagrees, the government can override the recommendation by Order in Council (a decision of the Governor-General acting on the advice of Cabinet). Under

LGOIMA, the equivalent power is held by the local authority itself: it can override the Ombudsman's recommendation by formal resolution. This resolution must be recorded in writing, published in the Gazette, publicly notified in a local newspaper, and must set out the reasons for the decision, the grounds in support of those reasons, and the source and purport of any advice relied upon. These transparency requirements are more extensive than those for the OIA override. A local authority cannot contract out of these requirements, as the court confirmed in a case where a company argued that a confidentiality agreement prevented a council from disclosing information.

Charging restrictions. Under the OIA, the Government's Charging Guidelines set the framework for charges. Under LGOIMA, regulations may be made prescribing maximum charges, and where such regulations exist, no local authority may charge more than the prescribed amount. In the absence of regulations (and none have been made to date), charges must be "reasonable," which the Ombudsman has interpreted as requiring consistency with the Government's Charging Guidelines. In practice, some councils have adopted their own charging policies through their annual plans, with rates that vary by staff seniority. The Ombudsman has found such variable rates to be unreasonable, and has directed councils to bring their charges into line with the standard guidelines.

The Ombudsman's reporting power. Under the OIA, if an agency fails to comply with the Ombudsman's recommendation and the executive override is not invoked, the Ombudsman can report directly to the Prime Minister or to Parliament. Under LGOIMA, the Ombudsman's equivalent power is different: the Ombudsman may require the principal administrative officer to make a summary of the Ombudsman's report available for free public inspection for four weeks, with public notification at the authority's expense. This process is designed to bring public pressure to bear on the local authority through local scrutiny rather than through parliamentary accountability.

Access to Local Authority Meetings and Agendas

One of the most distinctive features of LGOIMA is that it goes well beyond information requests. Part VII of the Act extends the principles of open government to local authority meetings, aligning the reasons for closing meetings to the public with those for withholding official information. This is a significant additional tool for anyone seeking to understand and participate in local government decision-making.

The right to attend meetings. The core of Part VII is the right of the public to attend meetings of local authorities and their committees. Every meeting must be open to the public unless there are grounds for excluding them. The grounds for exclusion mirror the withholding grounds for official information: a meeting can go into "public excluded" session only if one of the LGOIMA section 7 grounds (or the section 6 grounds of maintenance of the law or safety of any person) applies to the information that will be discussed. The local authority must pass a resolution to exclude the public, and that resolution must identify the general subject matter, the reason for exclusion, and the relevant ground under the Act.

Public notification of meetings. Local authorities must publicly notify their meeting schedules, giving the public reasonable advance notice of when and where meetings will be held. This notification must appear in a local newspaper (or, where none exists, on notices posted in public places). For ordinary meetings, at least 10 working days' notice must be given to members.

Availability of agendas and reports. Agendas and associated reports for meetings must be made available to the public at the local authority's main office, service delivery centres, and libraries at least two working days before the meeting. This is a powerful right: it means that the public can see what the council will be considering before the meeting takes place, and can prepare submissions, attend the relevant parts of the meeting, or make follow-up LGOIMA requests for underlying material.

However, local authorities may withhold items from the publicly available agenda if there is good reason to do so under the withholding grounds. In practice, this means that items to be discussed in "public excluded" session will typically not have their reports publicly available, although the agenda must still indicate the general nature of the business to be transacted.

Availability of minutes. The public is entitled to inspect and obtain copies of the minutes of any meeting (or part of a meeting) at which they were entitled to be present. Minutes of public-excluded sessions are not automatically available, although they may be requested as official information under the ordinary LGOIMA request process.

For requesters, the meetings regime is a valuable complement to the information request process. If you know that a council is about to consider a matter you are interested in, you can obtain the meeting papers in advance, attend the meeting, and then use LGOIMA requests to follow up on any information that was not made publicly available. The meeting papers themselves often identify the reports, briefings, and correspondence that underlie the council's decision-making, giving you precise targets for your LGOIMA requests.

Common Types of Local Government Information

Local authorities hold a vast range of information that is of practical interest to residents, ratepayers, businesses, community groups, and researchers. Understanding the types of information that councils hold, and where they are likely to be found, will help you craft effective LGOIMA requests.

Resource consents and planning information. Councils process resource consent applications under the Resource Management Act 1991. The information generated includes applications (with supporting plans, assessments of environmental effects, and expert reports), submissions from the public, officers' reports, hearing panel decisions, and any conditions imposed. Much of this information is publicly available as a matter of course, because the resource consent process is itself public. But LGOIMA can be used to access internal council communications about consent applications, pre-application discussions between applicants and council staff, and legal advice obtained by the council on planning matters.

Rates information. Councils set and collect rates, and the information generated includes rating valuations, rates assessments, rates arrears data, and policy documents about rating methodologies. Individual rating information for specific properties is generally available, but aggregated data about rating patterns or arrears may need to be requested.

Contracts and procurement. Councils enter into contracts for services ranging from road maintenance to waste collection to IT systems. LGOIMA can be used to access contract documents, tender evaluation reports, cost estimates, and performance reports. Commercial sensitivity (section 7(2)(b)) and negotiations (section 7(2)(i)) are commonly invoked in response to requests for this type of information, but the Ombudsman has been clear that the mere existence of a commercial relationship does not justify withholding. The specific prejudice must be identified, and the public interest in accountability for the expenditure of public funds weighs heavily in favour of release.

Meeting minutes and reports to council. As discussed above, minutes of public meetings are available as of right. Reports prepared by council officers for consideration by elected members are typically available as meeting papers, but internal drafts, earlier versions, and supporting analysis may need to be requested separately. Free and frank opinions (section 7(2)(f)(i)) is sometimes invoked in relation to draft reports or internal advice that preceded the final report to council, but the same principles apply as under the OIA: factual and background material should not be caught, and the passage of time diminishes the case for withholding.

Correspondence and communications. Councils generate significant volumes of correspondence with residents, ratepayers, businesses, government agencies, and other stakeholders. This includes complaint files, consultation responses, correspondence about building consents and code compliance, and communications between council staff and elected members about council business.

Financial information. Councils are required to prepare annual plans, long-term plans, and annual reports, all of which are publicly available. But LGOIMA can be used to access the underlying financial data, internal budget analyses, financial forecasts, and reports on financial performance that inform these public documents.

Council-controlled organisation information. Many councils have established council-controlled organisations (CCOs) to carry out specific functions, such as managing water infrastructure, operating ports, or running community facilities. CCOs are themselves subject to LGOIMA, and requests can be made directly to them. However, requesters should be aware that the boundary between a council and its CCOs can create gaps: the council may say the information is held by the CCO, and the CCO may say it is operational and not subject to the same level of disclosure. If you encounter this, the transfer provisions of LGOIMA apply, and you can also make parallel requests to both entities.

Challenges Specific to Local Government

Requesting from local government presents some practical challenges that are less common (or less acute) when requesting from central government agencies.

Smaller organisations with limited expertise. New Zealand has 78 local authorities, ranging from large metropolitan councils with substantial legal and communications teams to small district councils with only a handful of staff. The smaller councils may not have dedicated OIA/LGOIMA teams, may not have in-house legal advice readily available, and may have less experience with the legislation. This can cut both ways: smaller councils may be more willing to release information informally and without the bureaucratic process that larger agencies follow, but they may also be more likely to make errors in applying the withholding grounds, to miss the statutory time limits, or to be uncertain about their obligations.

If you are requesting from a smaller council and encounter difficulties, a polite reference to the Ombudsman's published guidance can be helpful. Many smaller councils are genuinely trying to comply but lack the institutional knowledge that larger agencies have built up over decades. The Ombudsman's office can also provide informal guidance to councils that are unsure how to handle a request, and you can suggest that the council contact the Ombudsman's office if it needs assistance.

Elected members and political dynamics. Local government is directly democratic in a way that central government is not. Elected councillors are members of the decision-making body, they are often closely connected to the communities they serve, and they may have strong personal views about whether particular information should be released. Under LGOIMA, elected members do not make first-instance decisions on requests (that is the role of the principal administrative officer), but their influence can still be felt. Elected members may pressure staff to withhold information that they consider politically sensitive. They may also be the subject of requests, which creates tension when a councillor's own communications or conduct are at issue.

The legal position is clear: the decision on a LGOIMA request is made by the chief executive or their delegate, not by elected members. If you suspect that a decision has been improperly influenced by elected members, this is a matter you can raise with the Ombudsman. Elected members are, however, directly involved in two related processes: the decision to exclude the public from meetings (which requires a resolution of the council or committee), and the decision to override an Ombudsman recommendation (which also requires a formal resolution).

The overlap between LGOIMA and other local government transparency requirements. Local government in New Zealand operates under multiple transparency regimes. The Local Government Act 2002 imposes extensive requirements for consultation, public reporting, and financial transparency. The Resource Management Act 1991 has its own notification and submission processes. The Local Authorities (Members'

Interests) Act 1968 regulates conflicts of interest. These overlapping regimes mean that a significant amount of local government information is already publicly available through channels other than LGOIMA. Before making a LGOIMA request, check the council's website for meeting agendas and minutes, annual plans, long-term plans, annual reports, consultation documents, and resource consent files. Many councils also publish their policies, bylaws, and key contracts online.

However, the existence of other transparency mechanisms does not limit your right to make LGOIMA requests. LGOIMA provides access to information that may not be captured by other disclosure requirements, including internal correspondence, draft documents, legal advice, financial analysis, and communications between staff and elected members.

Charging practices. As noted above, some councils have adopted their own charging policies that depart from the Government's Charging Guidelines. If you receive a charge notification from a council that seems out of line with the standard guidelines (for example, charges at variable rates depending on staff seniority, or charges for activities that should not be charged for), challenge it. The Ombudsman has repeatedly found council charging practices to be unreasonable when they exceed the guidelines.

Information management. Some smaller councils have less sophisticated information management systems than central government agencies. Records may be held in paper files rather than electronic document management systems, email archives may be incomplete, and the institutional memory of staff may be the primary means of locating older information. This can make searches slower and less reliable. If you receive a "not held" response from a council and you believe the information should exist, ask about the searches that were conducted and suggest specific places or systems that might be checked, as discussed in Chapter 16.

Practical Advice for LGOIMA Requesters

Several practical principles will help you get the most out of LGOIMA.

First, use the publicly available material as your starting point. Council meeting agendas, minutes, annual plans, and published reports are freely available and will often answer your questions without the need for a formal request. They will also help you identify the specific documents or information you want to request, allowing you to make focused, effective requests rather than broad ones.

Second, use the meetings regime as a complement to the request process. If a matter is coming before the council, obtain the meeting papers in advance, attend the meeting, and note any references to documents or information that are not publicly available. These references give you precise targets for follow-up LGOIMA requests.

Third, be aware of the council's structure. Many councils delegate functions to committees, subcommittees, community boards, and council-controlled organisations. Information about a particular topic may be held by any of these bodies. If you are not sure where to direct your request, start with the main council and ask to be directed to the right place. The transfer provisions of LGOIMA apply between council bodies just as they do between central government agencies.

Fourth, engage constructively with council staff. Local government is closer to the community than central government, and the relationship between requesters and council staff is often more personal and more direct. A phone call or email to the relevant council officer can sometimes resolve your query without the need for a formal request, and can help you frame a request effectively if one is needed.

Fifth, do not be deterred by the size or informality of a smaller council. The legal obligations under LGOIMA are the same regardless of the council's size. The principle of availability applies. The statutory time limits apply. The Ombudsman's review jurisdiction applies. If a council fails to meet its obligations, the same complaint process is available to you as it would be for a request to a central government department.

Sixth, remember that LGOIMA gives you rights that go beyond the OIA. The open meetings regime, the public availability of agendas and reports, the broader eligibility to make requests, and the public nature of the override process all provide additional tools for holding local government accountable. Used together, these tools give requesters a comprehensive framework for understanding and scrutinising the decisions that affect their communities.

CHAPTER 19

Special Types of Requests

The OIA and LGOIMA contain three provisions that go beyond the ordinary right to request official information. These provisions create enhanced rights of access to specific categories of information that are fundamental to transparent and accountable decision-making: internal rules and guidelines for decision-making (section 22 OIA / section 21 LGOIMA), statements of reasons for decisions affecting individuals (section 23 OIA / section 22 LGOIMA), and personal information held about corporate entities (Part 4 of both Acts).

What makes these provisions special is not just the type of information they cover, but the strength of the right they confer. Each provision establishes a right of access that is more robust than the ordinary Part 2 right, with a significantly narrower set of grounds on which requests can be refused. In particular, two of the most commonly invoked withholding grounds under the ordinary regime, free and frank opinions and legal professional privilege, cannot be used to refuse requests under these special provisions. This is a deliberate design choice: the framers of the legislation recognised that the information covered by these provisions is so central to individual rights and government accountability that the usual range of withholding justifications should not apply.

Many requesters, and some agencies, are unaware of these provisions or do not understand the enhanced rights they confer. This chapter explains each provision in detail, from the requester's perspective, and offers practical guidance on how to use them effectively.

Requests for Internal Rules and Guidelines for Decision Making

The Enhanced Right of Access

Section 22 of the OIA (section 21 of LGOIMA) provides a right of access, on request, to any document held by an agency which contains policies, principles, rules, or guidelines in accordance with which decisions or recommendations are made in respect of any person or body of persons in their personal capacity. The committee that recommended the enactment of the OIA described this category of information as "informal administrative law" or "internal law": the body of rules and criteria applied by agencies in making decisions affecting the rights, privileges, or liabilities of individuals.

The rationale for this provision is the principle that individuals have a right to know the law that does or may affect them personally. If an agency is making decisions about you, whether about your visa application, your benefit entitlement, your licence, your regulatory compliance, or your contract, you are entitled to know the rules by which those decisions are being made. Section 22 ensures that people can understand and, if necessary, challenge the decisions made about them, and that agencies can be held accountable for consistency and fairness.

The scope of section 22 is broad. "Document" is defined to include any form of record: hardcopy or electronic, including manuals, circulars, memoranda, spreadsheets, and material stored on computer systems. "Internal decision making rules" encompasses not just formal published policies but also informal guidance, desk instructions, interpretation bulletins, decision trees, scoring matrices, risk assessment frameworks, and precedent decisions that function as guidelines. The Ombudsman has found that the critical question is whether the document functions as an aid to decision-making that affects people personally, not whether the agency has formally designated it as a "policy" or "guideline."

Importantly, the decision or recommendation need not affect the requester themselves. It is sufficient that the decision affects any person or group in their personal capacity. This means that advocacy organisations, community groups, lawyers, and researchers can all use section 22 to access decision-making rules, not just individuals who are personally affected.

The Limited Grounds for Refusal

Because section 22 creates a right of access, the grounds for refusing a request are significantly narrower than under Part 2 of the Act. The conclusive reasons that can apply are: security, defence, and international relations (OIA only); confidential information provided by another country or international organisation (OIA only); maintenance of the law; and personal safety. The good reasons that can apply (subject to the public interest test) are: privacy; disclosure of a trade secret or unreasonable prejudice to the commercial position of a third party; information subject to an obligation of confidence; commercial activities; and negotiations.

The critical exclusions are what make section 22 so powerful for requesters. Free and frank opinions (section 9(2)(g)(i) OIA / section 7(2)(f)(i) LGOIMA) cannot be invoked. Legal professional privilege (section 9(2)(h) OIA / section 7(2)(g) LGOIMA) cannot be invoked. These are two of the most commonly used withholding grounds under Part 2, and their exclusion from section 22 means that agencies cannot refuse to disclose their decision-making rules on the basis that they contain candid internal advice or legal analysis. The Ombudsman's guidance is explicit: agencies should not expect to be able to withhold information in response to a section 22 request on these grounds.

The administrative reasons for refusal found in section 18 of the OIA (section 17 of LGOIMA) do not apply to section 22 requests either. This means that "substantial collation or research" and "frivolous, vexatious, or trivial" cannot be cited as reasons for refusing. However, if the volume of material is large, agencies can extend the time limit or impose a reasonable charge. On charging, the Ombudsman has noted that section 22 recognises a strong public interest in general availability of internal decision-making rules, which may make it unreasonable for one requester to bear the full cost of making them available. In one case, the Ombudsman found that it was unreasonable for the Customs Service to impose a substantial charge on a single requester for access to policies on border searches, and encouraged Customs to make such information broadly available to the public online.

Practical Examples

Section 22 is useful in a wide range of contexts.

Immigration. Immigration New Zealand publishes its Operational Manual, but there may be additional internal guidance, interpretation notes, or practice directions that are not publicly available. A section 22 request can access these materials. In one case, the Ombudsman found that INZ's published manuals and circulars fell within section 22, while an internal "mind map" used to draft policies did not, because it was not an aid to decision-making in its own right.

Benefit eligibility. Work and Income New Zealand publishes its Manuals and Procedures, but supplementary guidance, training materials, and desk instructions used by case managers in assessing benefit applications may not be publicly available. A section 22 request can access any document that functions as a guide for decisions about individual entitlement.

Prosecution guidelines. Regulatory agencies such as the Commerce Commission, the Financial Markets Authority, WorkSafe, and regional councils apply prosecution guidelines when deciding whether to bring enforcement proceedings. These guidelines affect individuals directly and fall squarely within section 22.

Customs procedures. As the Ombudsman's case involving the Customs Service illustrates, policies about how searches are conducted and the rights of people being searched are accessible under section 22.

Dispute resolution procedures. Where an agency has internal procedures for settling disputes (such as the Customs Service's procedures for disputes involving seized vehicles), these are accessible under section 22 even if the agency has not formally labelled them as decision-making guidelines.

Requests for Reasons for Decisions

When This Right Arises

Section 23 of the OIA (section 22 of LGOIMA) gives any affected person the right to request a written statement of reasons for any decision or recommendation made about them in their personal capacity by a public service agency, Minister, or organisation subject to the Act. The request must be made within a "reasonable time" of the decision or recommendation.

The significance of this provision is hard to overstate. The Eagles, Taggart, and Liddell text describes it as remarkable for both its breadth of coverage and specificity of requirement. It places a duty on any decision-maker covered by the OIA to provide, on request, a formal written statement that explains not just the outcome but the reasoning process.

The right is triggered whenever a "decision or recommendation" is made "in respect of" a person "in their personal capacity." This covers decisions that directly affect you (a decision on your application, your complaint, your employment, your regulatory status), as well as recommendations made about you (a recommendation that your funding be discontinued, that your licence not be renewed, that enforcement action be taken). The decision or recommendation need not be final: preliminary recommendations and assessments can also be caught.

"Personal capacity" distinguishes decisions about you as an individual from decisions about policy or general matters. If an agency decides to change a policy that affects thousands of people, that is not a decision about you in your personal capacity. But if an agency applies that policy to your individual case and reaches a particular outcome, that application is a decision about you.

What the Statement of Reasons Must Contain

A section 23 statement must be in writing and must include three elements.

First, the findings on material issues of fact. A material fact is one that is central to the decision and can affect its outcome. If a fact is relied upon, it must be stated. If a matter is considered and a finding of fact is made about it, that finding must be stated. When a finding of fact is inferred from other facts (for example, a finding about the nature of a relationship inferred from living arrangements), the statement should set out both the primary facts and the process of inference. The Ombudsman's guidance emphasises that findings of fact should be distinguished from subjective judgments or opinions, and that where a judgment or opinion is based on facts, those underlying facts should be set out.

Second, a reference to the information on which the findings were based. This means identifying the specific evidence that supported each material finding, not simply listing all the documents that were before the decision-maker. The information must be described in a way that makes it readily identifiable, for instance by referring to the author, date, and subject of a report or letter. Only a reference is required, not a copy of the information, although the agency may choose to provide copies and the requester can always seek the underlying information through a separate Part 2 request.

Third, the reasons for the decision or recommendation. This means the actual and real reasons, not a post hoc rationalisation prepared with the benefit of hindsight. The statement must contain all steps of reasoning, linking the facts to the outcome, so that the requester can understand how the decision was reached. The Court of Appeal has held that the reasons must be proper and adequate, dealing with the point in contention. If the reader is likely to be left guessing as to why the decision was reached, the statement of reasons is not good enough.

The Ombudsman's guidance notes that simply providing a copy of an underlying report and saying "my decision was based on this report" is not sufficient. The three elements must be supplied: the findings, the references to evidence, and the reasons. Even where a decision is made by adopting someone else's recommendation, the decision-maker must explain their own reasoning.

The Limited Grounds for Refusal

As with section 22, the grounds for refusing a section 23 request are significantly narrower than under Part 2. The applicable withholding grounds are: security, defence, and international relations; confidential information provided by another country or international organisation; maintenance of the law; personal safety; and disclosure of a trade secret or unreasonable prejudice to the commercial position of a third party (subject to the public interest test).

Again, the critical exclusions are free and frank opinions and legal professional privilege. An agency cannot refuse to explain its reasoning on the basis that the reasons contain candid internal opinions or legal advice. This is a deliberate and powerful feature of section 23: it prevents agencies from hiding behind claims of frankness or privilege to avoid explaining their decisions to the people affected by them.

There are also limited exceptions to the duty to provide a reference to the underlying information. The most significant relates to "evaluative material": if the information is evaluative or opinion material compiled solely for the purpose of determining a person's suitability or eligibility, and disclosure would breach an express or implied promise of confidentiality made to the supplier of the information, the agency may withhold the reference. This exception protects confidential references in employment and similar contexts, but it is narrow: it applies only to evaluative material (not to facts), only to material compiled for the sole purpose of the relevant decision, and only where a genuine promise of confidentiality was made.

Practical Examples

Employment decisions. If a government department declines to appoint you to a position, you can request a statement of reasons under section 23. The statement must explain the criteria applied, the findings about your qualifications and performance against those criteria, and the reasons for preferring another candidate. The agency cannot withhold this on the basis of free and frank opinions about your suitability.

Regulatory decisions. If a regulatory body declines your application for a licence, imposes conditions, or takes enforcement action against you, section 23 gives you the right to understand the factual basis and reasoning behind that decision. This is particularly valuable where the decision involves the exercise of discretion, because it requires the agency to explain not just what it decided but why.

Funding decisions. If a government agency declines your organisation's application for funding or discontinues an existing grant, a section 23 request can require the agency to explain its assessment of your application and its reasons for the adverse decision.

Procurement decisions. If you tender for a government contract and are not selected, section 23 entitles you to a statement of reasons explaining how the tender was evaluated, what findings were made about your bid, and why another tenderer was preferred.

Benefit decisions. If Work and Income declines a benefit application or imposes conditions, section 23 requires the agency to explain its findings and reasoning in writing. This is a complement to the section 22 right to access the decision-making rules: together, sections 22 and 23 allow you to understand both the rules and how they were applied to your case.

Requests by Corporate Entities for Their Personal Information

Part 4 of the OIA (and the equivalent provisions of LGOIMA) gives corporate entities the right to request any information that an agency holds about them. This is the corporate equivalent of the individual's right to access personal information under the Privacy Act. Under the OIA, this right can be exercised by bodies corporate incorporated in New Zealand or those that have a place of business in New Zealand. Under LGOIMA, there are no eligibility restrictions, consistent with the broader access provisions of that Act.

The term "personal information" in the corporate context means information about the corporate entity itself, not about its directors or employees as individuals (their information is protected by the Privacy Act). It covers information about the company's dealings with the agency, its compliance record, assessments of its performance, information gathered about it in the course of regulatory activity, and any other information that relates to the entity.

The right under Part 4 is a right of access to any information about the corporate entity that can be "readily retrieved." This means information that the agency can find without disproportionate effort, not information that is scattered across multiple unrelated files and would require substantial work to compile.

As with sections 22 and 23, the grounds for refusing a Part 4 request are more limited than those available under Part 2. Importantly, free and frank opinions cannot be invoked. The applicable withholding grounds include: the conclusive reasons in section 6 (section 6 of LGOIMA); disclosure of a trade secret or unreasonable prejudice to the commercial position of a third party (subject to the public interest test); and unwarranted disclosure of the affairs of another person.

The "unwarranted disclosure" ground requires a balancing exercise. The agency must weigh the corporate entity's right of access (including why it needs the information) against the privacy or confidentiality interests of the other person whose affairs would be disclosed. To get this balance right, agencies can consider partial release or providing the information in an alternative form, such as a summary.

Part 4 also protects "evaluative material" in the same way as section 23: evaluative or opinion material compiled solely for the purpose of determining the entity's suitability for contracts, awards, or benefits can be withheld if disclosure would breach an express or implied promise of confidentiality to the supplier. But only the evaluative component is protected; the facts on which the evaluation was based are not.

Practical Uses of Part 4

Procurement. A company that has tendered for a government contract can use Part 4 to access the information the agency holds about its tender, including evaluation reports and assessments. This complements a section 23 request for reasons for the decision not to award the contract.

Regulatory compliance. A company subject to regulatory oversight can use Part 4 to access the information an agency holds about its compliance history, including inspection reports, compliance assessments, and correspondence about its regulatory status.

Investigations. A corporate entity that is or has been the subject of an agency investigation can use Part 4 to access information gathered during the investigation, subject to any applicable withholding grounds (such as maintenance of the law if the investigation is ongoing).

Due diligence. Companies involved in mergers, acquisitions, or other transactions may use Part 4 to access information that government agencies hold about them, as part of their due diligence processes.

Using These Provisions Together

The three special provisions described in this chapter are designed to work together. Section 22 gives you access to the rules by which decisions are made. Section 23 gives you access to the reasons for a specific decision about you. Part 4 gives corporate entities access to the information an agency holds about them. Used in combination, they provide a comprehensive framework for understanding and challenging government decision-making.

A practical example illustrates how the three provisions interact. Suppose a company applies for a government contract and is unsuccessful. It can use section 22 to obtain the procurement guidelines and evaluation criteria that the agency applied. It can use section 23 to obtain a statement of reasons for the decision, including the findings of fact about its tender and the reasons for preferring another bidder. And it can use Part 4 to access any other information the agency holds about it, such as performance assessments from previous contracts or internal correspondence about its tender.

For individual requesters (as opposed to corporate entities), the combination of section 22 and section 23 is particularly powerful. If you have been affected by a government decision, you can first use section 22 to understand the rules that should have been applied, and then use section 23 to see whether the agency actually followed those rules in your case. Any gap between the stated rules and the actual reasoning may form the basis of a challenge, either through the agency's own review processes, through the Ombudsman, or through the courts.

One final point: if your request falls within one of these special provisions but the agency treats it as an ordinary Part 2 request, the agency may apply withholding grounds (such as free and frank opinions or legal professional privilege) that would not be available if the request were properly categorised. If this happens, draw the agency's attention to the relevant section. If the agency persists in its refusal, complain to the Ombudsman, who will assess the request under the correct provision. The Ombudsman has found that agencies sometimes fail to recognise that a request engages section 22 or section 23, and has directed disclosure in cases where the agency's refusal was based on withholding grounds that do not apply to these enhanced-right provisions.

CHAPTER 20

Using the OIA for Investigations and Research

The earlier chapters of this book explain the OIA's legal framework and practical mechanics. This chapter is different. It is about strategy: how to use the OIA as a tool for investigation, research, advocacy, litigation, and business intelligence. It draws on the practices of the journalists, researchers, lawyers, advocates, and businesspeople who use the Act most intensively, and offers practical guidance that goes well beyond the mechanics of making a single request.

The OIA is not just a system for obtaining individual documents. Used thoughtfully, it is a method for building understanding of how government works, for holding agencies accountable, for informing public debate, and for advancing the interests of clients, communities, and the public. The requesters who get the most value from the Act are those who approach it strategically, not as a one-off transaction but as part of a broader information-gathering effort.

Strategies for Journalists

Journalists are among the most intensive users of the OIA, and the ones whose experience of it is most heavily shaped by political dynamics. Research into the Act's administration has found that requests from journalists receive closer scrutiny, take longer to process, and are more likely to involve ministerial consultation than requests from other types of requesters. This is the environment in which journalists must operate, and effective strategies are essential.

Building a story through sequential requests. The most effective journalists do not rely on a single broad request to produce a story. Instead, they build their understanding through a sequence of targeted requests, each informed by what they learned from the previous one. The first request in a sequence is often a scene-setter: a request for briefings, reports, or correspondence on a topic, designed to map the terrain and identify the key documents and decision points. Subsequent requests drill into the specifics: the minutes of a particular meeting, the legal advice on a particular issue, the correspondence between specific officials about a specific decision. This sequential approach avoids the problems associated with overly broad requests (charges, delays, refusals on substantial collation grounds) while steadily building a comprehensive picture.

Using proactive releases as leads. Proactively released Cabinet papers, regulatory impact statements, briefings, and OIA responses published on agency websites or through fyi.org.nz are a rich source of leads. Every proactively released document contains references to other documents: earlier briefings, supporting analysis, legal advice, consultation records, draft versions. These references are, in effect, a catalogue of information that exists and can be requested. Experienced journalists routinely scan proactive releases not just for the information they contain but for the information they point to.

Handling political sensitivity. Journalists should assume that any request on a politically sensitive topic will be notified to the Minister's office and possibly subject to consultation. Build this into your timeline. If your story is time-sensitive, consider making your request to the department (which has better systems and is less likely to hold a request up for political reasons) rather than to the Minister. If your request is transferred to the Minister, be aware that the clock restarts and plan accordingly. And remember that once the statutory time limit passes, you can complain to the Ombudsman. The mere fact that a complaint has been made often accelerates the process.

Managing the timing of releases. Some agencies time the release of OIA responses to minimise media impact, for example by releasing late on a Friday afternoon. Experienced journalists anticipate this and build it into their workflow. If you receive a large release at an inconvenient time, the information is not going anywhere. Take the time you need to read it carefully rather than rushing to publish.

Cross-referencing with other sources. The OIA is one tool among several. Parliamentary questions, select committee inquiries, annual reports, Estimates hearings, and public registers all provide information that can be cross-referenced with OIA releases. Several experienced requesters interviewed for research on the Act described using parliamentary questions and OIA requests in tandem, with parliamentary questions used to identify topics or documents and OIA requests used to obtain the underlying material. Information released to one person also circulates rapidly through professional networks, and monitoring fyi.org.nz and other public archives can reveal what others have already obtained.

Strategies for Researchers

Academic and policy researchers use the OIA differently from journalists. Their timelines are usually longer, their information needs are more systematic, and their relationship with the agencies they study is often more collaborative. But they face their own distinctive challenges, particularly around large data requests and the interface between the OIA and the Privacy Act.

Academic research. If you are conducting academic research that will involve multiple OIA requests to the same agency, consider approaching the agency informally before making your first request. Explain your research project, describe the types of information you will need, and ask whether the agency would be willing to work with you to identify the most efficient way of providing it. Research into the OIA has found that agencies are often more accommodating of researchers who are known and trusted, and who are clearly working outside the political realm. This does not mean you have fewer rights than other requesters, but it does mean that a constructive relationship can make the process smoother and faster.

Policy research. Policy researchers often need information that spans multiple agencies or multiple time periods. Develop a requesting strategy that recognises the practical limits of the system. Rather than making one enormous request, consider making a series of requests, each focused on a manageable slice of the material. Use the early responses to refine your later requests. If you need comparative data across agencies, standardise your requests so that the responses are comparable.

Data requests. If you need quantitative data rather than documents, specify this clearly in your request. Agencies hold large amounts of data in databases and information systems, and a well-targeted data request can be much easier for the agency to fulfil than a request for "all documents" on a topic. Specify the data fields you need, the time period, and the format you want. Request the data in a reusable electronic format (see below) so that you can analyse it directly rather than re-entering figures from a PDF or printout.

The interface with the Privacy Act. If your research involves information about identifiable individuals, you may encounter the boundary between the OIA and the Privacy Act. The OIA covers official information in general; the Privacy Act covers personal information about natural persons. If you are seeking aggregated or anonymised data, the OIA is the right route. If you are seeking information that identifies specific individuals, the privacy withholding ground (section 9(2)(a)) will apply, and you may need to consider whether the Privacy Act provides an alternative means of access (for the individuals concerned, not for you as a researcher). In some cases, agencies can release data with personal identifiers removed, which avoids the privacy issue while giving you the information you need.

Strategies for Advocates and NGOs

Advocacy organisations and non-governmental organisations use the OIA to inform their submissions, monitor government performance, and hold agencies accountable for their decisions. For these requesters, the OIA is a tool for democratic participation, and the strategies that work best are those that connect OIA requests to broader advocacy objectives.

Informing submissions. When a government agency is consulting on a proposed policy, regulation, or plan, OIA requests can access the underlying analysis, options papers, cost-benefit assessments, and legal advice that informed the proposal. This material is invaluable for preparing informed submissions, because it allows you to engage with the agency's own reasoning rather than speculating about what lies behind a proposal. Time your requests to allow for the statutory processing period: make them early in the consultation process so that you have the material before the submission deadline.

Monitoring government performance. NGOs that work in a particular policy area can use the OIA systematically to monitor how agencies are performing their functions. Regular requests for performance data, complaint statistics, inspection reports, and internal audit findings can build a longitudinal picture of agency performance that would not otherwise be available. Consider establishing a regular requesting rhythm (for example, quarterly requests for the same categories of data) so that you can track trends over time.

Holding agencies accountable. The OIA is at its most powerful when it reveals a gap between what an agency says it is doing and what it is actually doing. Requests for internal correspondence, meeting minutes, and decision records can test whether agencies are following their own policies, complying with their legal obligations, and acting consistently. Use section 22 (internal decision-making rules) to obtain the agency's own standards, and then use Part 2 requests to test whether those standards are being met in practice.

Building coalitions. Information obtained under the OIA can be shared with other organisations, media, and the public. There is no restriction on what you do with information once it has been released to you. Consider publishing OIA responses on your website, sharing them with journalists, and using them in public advocacy. The more widely the information circulates, the greater its impact.

Managing the cost. NGOs often operate on limited budgets, and charges for OIA requests can be a significant barrier. If you are charged, consider arguing for remission on public interest grounds: the Ombudsman's guidance recognises that the public interest in the availability of information may make it unreasonable for a public interest group to bear the full cost. Some agencies have internal policies on charging public interest groups, and it is worth asking about this.

Strategies for Lawyers

Lawyers use the OIA in the context of litigation, regulatory proceedings, and client advice. Their use of the Act raises distinctive issues about the relationship between OIA requests and formal legal processes.

OIA requests as pre-litigation investigation. The OIA can be used to establish the factual foundation for a legal claim before proceedings are filed. By requesting the agency's file, correspondence, and decision records, a lawyer can assess whether the client has a case and identify the key documents. Research into the OIA has found that some agencies recognise this use and respond accordingly, while others find it challenging, particularly when OIA requests are seen as an alternative to the formal discovery process.

The relationship between OIA and discovery. If litigation is already underway or clearly imminent, the agency may argue that the OIA request should be declined in favour of the discovery process. There is no explicit provision in the OIA for this, and the Ombudsman has not recognised "pending litigation" as a ground for refusal. However, the practical dynamics may be affected: agencies that know they are facing litigation may apply the withholding grounds more conservatively, and may invoke legal professional privilege (section 9(2)(h)) more readily. Be aware that the OIA and discovery overlap but are not identical: discovery may produce a wider class of documents, but the OIA can be faster and does not require proceedings to have been filed.

Regulatory proceedings. Lawyers acting for clients in regulatory proceedings (resource consent hearings, financial markets investigations, competition inquiries) can use the OIA to access the regulator's internal analysis, correspondence, and decision-making records. Section 22 (internal decision-making rules) and section 23 (reasons for decisions) are particularly useful in this context, as discussed in Chapter 19. The limited withholding grounds available under those provisions mean that the regulator cannot refuse to explain its reasoning by citing free and frank opinions or legal privilege.

Client advice. Lawyers advising clients on their obligations or exposure can use the OIA to access the agency's interpretation of the relevant legislation, its compliance policies, and its enforcement priorities. This information may not be publicly available but is accessible under the OIA, and particularly under section 22 if it constitutes internal decision-making rules.

Using information strategically. Lawyers should be aware that information obtained under the OIA is in the public domain once released. If your client's strategy depends on the information remaining confidential, the OIA may not be the right tool. Consider whether informal engagement with the agency, or the formal discovery process (which can involve confidentiality orders), would better serve the client's interests.

Strategies for Businesses

Businesses use the OIA in the context of procurement, regulation, and competitive intelligence. Their use raises issues about commercial sensitivity and the interface between the requester's commercial interests and the interests of third parties.

Procurement. Businesses that tender for government contracts can use the OIA to access information about the procurement process, including evaluation criteria, assessment reports, and the reasons for the decision. Section 22 provides access to the procurement guidelines, section 23 provides access to the reasons for the decision, and Part 4 provides access to information about the company itself. Together, these provisions give unsuccessful tenderers a comprehensive picture of why they were not selected, which can inform future bids or, in extreme cases, a legal challenge to the procurement decision.

Regulation. Businesses subject to government regulation can use the OIA to understand how the regulator operates: what its compliance priorities are, how it interprets the legislation, what thresholds it applies for enforcement action, and how it assesses risk. Much of this information constitutes internal decision-making rules under section 22 and is accessible with limited grounds for refusal.

Competitor intelligence. The OIA can be used to access information about the regulatory compliance, performance, or dealings of competitors, to the extent that this information is held by government agencies. However, the commercial sensitivity withholding ground (section 9(2)(b)) may apply to protect the commercial position of the third party, and the confidentiality ground (section 9(2)(ba)) may apply if the information was provided in confidence. The agency will typically consult the third party before deciding whether to release. If you are seeking commercially sensitive information about a competitor, be prepared for a longer processing time and a greater likelihood of partial withholding.

Working with Large Volumes of Released Information

If your request produces a large release (hundreds or thousands of pages), effective management of the material is essential. Here are some practical approaches.

Triage the material. Do not try to read everything from start to finish. Scan the release for the most important documents first: decision memos, briefings to Ministers, legal advice, and correspondence between senior officials. Background material, routine administrative emails, and duplicates can be set aside for later review.

Create an index. For a large release, create a simple index or spreadsheet that records the date, author, recipient, subject, and key content of each document. This will allow you to find specific documents quickly, identify gaps in the record, and track the chronology of events.

Look for what is missing. A large release can be as revealing for what it does not contain as for what it does. If the chronology shows a gap, or if a document refers to earlier advice or correspondence that was not included in the release, consider making a follow-up request specifically targeting the missing material.

Preserve the material. OIA responses are not archived by the agency for the requester's benefit. Keep your own copies, organised by date and topic. If you received the material electronically, back it up. If you received it on paper, consider scanning it for easier searching and storage.

Using Data Held by Agencies: Requesting in Reusable Electronic Formats

One of the most underused features of the OIA is the right to request information in your preferred format, including in reusable electronic formats. Section 16(1) of the OIA provides that information may be made available in a range of ways, and section 16(1A) confirms that this includes electronic form or electronic means. The agency must provide the information in the way you prefer unless doing so would impair efficient administration, be contrary to a legal duty, or prejudice the interests protected by the withholding grounds.

For data held in databases, spreadsheets, or information systems, requesting in electronic format has several advantages. It allows you to analyse the data directly rather than re-entering it from a printed document. It allows you to work with the data in spreadsheet or statistical software. And it avoids the costs and delays associated with printing, photocopying, and posting large volumes of paper.

When requesting data in electronic format, be specific about what you want. Specify the data fields, the time period, and the format (for example, CSV, Excel, or XML). If you are requesting statistical data that the agency compiles from individual records, make clear that you want the aggregated data, not individual records (which may raise privacy issues). If the agency holds the data in a database, ask whether it can run a report or extract matching your specifications.

The Ombudsman has confirmed that requesting information in electronic form when it has previously been supplied on paper is a legitimate new request, not a frivolous repeat. In one case, the Chief Ombudsman found that a requester who sought statistical information in electronic form after receiving it on paper was entitled to the electronic version, because the electronic format would allow the data to be properly analysed. The

Ombudsman also noted that this was a public interest consideration: the ability to analyse data enables informed responses to government policy initiatives.

Government data portals such as data.govt.nz, policedata.nz, and budget.govt.nz publish a growing volume of data in reusable formats. Before making a request, check whether the data you need is already available through these channels. If it is, you can save yourself and the agency the time and cost of processing a formal request. If the data is not available, your request may prompt the agency to consider making it available proactively for the benefit of future users.

A Note on Ethics and Responsibility

The OIA is a powerful tool, and with that power comes responsibility. Requesters who use the Act intensively, whether as journalists, researchers, advocates, lawyers, or businesspeople, should be mindful of several considerations.

First, the information you receive may contain personal details about individuals, commercially sensitive material about businesses, or operationally sensitive information about government activities. Handle it responsibly. The fact that information has been released to you does not mean it should be published or disseminated without thought about the consequences.

Second, agencies have finite resources. Large, complex, or frequent requests consume staff time and can affect the agency's ability to carry out its other functions, including responding to other requesters. This does not mean you should refrain from making the requests you need, but it does mean that making your requests as focused and efficient as possible serves everyone's interests, including your own.

Third, the OIA works best when it operates in a climate of reasonable trust between requesters and agencies. Requesters who engage constructively, who respond to consultation in good faith, and who acknowledge when agencies have been helpful contribute to a culture in which the Act is administered more effectively for everyone. The adversarial dynamics that research into the Act has documented, where suspicion and distrust drive both sides towards more defensive positions, are a cost that falls on all users of the system.

The goal of the OIA is to enable public participation, promote accountability, and protect information where necessary. Every requester who uses the Act thoughtfully and effectively strengthens that system and contributes to the quality of New Zealand's democracy.

CHAPTER 21

Proactive Release and Open Government

The OIA was designed around a model of individual requests: you ask an agency for specific information, and the agency decides whether to release it. That model remains central to the Act. But alongside it, a different way of making government information available has grown steadily over the past two decades. Proactive release, where agencies publish official information without waiting to be asked, is now a significant feature of New Zealand's information landscape. For requesters, understanding how proactive release works, what it covers, and where its limits lie is essential to using the OIA effectively.

The Growing Culture of Proactive Release in New Zealand

Proactive release is not a new idea. Government agencies have always published some information as a matter of course: annual reports, legislation, budget documents, policy statements, and media releases. What has changed is the scale, the expectations, and the infrastructure.

The shift towards proactive release has been driven by several factors. The internet has made publication cheap and instant. Political and public expectations of transparency have increased. International commitments, including New Zealand's membership of the Open Government Partnership, have created formal obligations to expand access to government information. And the practical experience of administering the OIA has demonstrated that proactive release can reduce the volume of individual requests by making commonly sought information available before anyone needs to ask for it.

The Ombudsman has been a consistent advocate for proactive release, describing it as consistent with the purpose of the OIA, which is to progressively increase the availability of official information to the people of New Zealand. The Ombudsman's office considers proactive release practices when conducting investigations into agencies' official information practices, and has published detailed guidance on good practice in this area.

Te Kawa Mataaho (the Public Service Commission) encourages agencies to establish internal policies and practices that support increased proactive release, including publishing appropriate OIA responses, in line with the OIA's purpose. The Commission reports every six months on the number of OIA responses published on agency websites, creating a degree of public accountability for agencies that lag behind.

The range of information now proactively released by government agencies is wide. Examples include data published on data.govt.nz, tender information on gets.govt.nz, budget information on budget.govt.nz, ministerial diaries on beehive.govt.nz, crime statistics on policedata.nz, decision summaries published by the Overseas Investment Office, rest home audit reports published by the Ministry of Health, advice to Ministers published by agencies such as the Ministry for the Environment and Statistics New Zealand, and research and commentary published by the Treasury.

For requesters, the practical significance of this cultural shift is substantial. A great deal of information that would once have required a formal OIA request is now available on agency websites, on government data portals, and through the FYI archive. Before you make a request, it is always worth checking whether the information is already publicly available. This saves time, avoids charges, and may give you what you need immediately.

Cabinet Office Requirements for Proactive Release of Cabinet Material

The most significant formal requirement for proactive release in New Zealand relates to Cabinet material. Cabinet Office circular CO 23 (4) sets out the updated requirements for proactive release of Cabinet papers and related material. These requirements apply to all government agencies that submit material to Cabinet.

Under the current requirements, agencies are expected to proactively release Cabinet papers and key advice papers within a specified timeframe after Cabinet decisions are made. Before publication, the material must be reviewed through a due diligence process. The Cabinet Office circular specifies that agencies should consider whether the document contains any information that would have been withheld if it had been requested under the OIA; the application of the principles in the Privacy Act 2020; considerations of national security and the protective security requirements; whether any other legislation restricts disclosure; and whether there is any potential civil or criminal liability that might result from publication.

The Cabinet Office requirements have had a transformative effect on the availability of policy material. Cabinet papers, regulatory impact statements, departmental advice to Ministers, and related documents are now routinely published on agency websites. For requesters interested in the development of government policy, this is an enormously valuable resource. You can often trace the evolution of a policy decision from the initial departmental advice through to the final Cabinet paper and minute, all without making a single OIA request.

However, the system has important limitations. Agencies have discretion over the timing and extent of redactions. Some agencies are more diligent than others in publishing material promptly. The quality and navigability of the published material varies significantly between agencies. And the requirements apply to Cabinet material specifically; they do not cover the broader range of official information that agencies hold, such as operational reports, internal correspondence, contractual documents, or data sets.

For requesters, the practical advice is to check agency websites for proactively released Cabinet material before making an OIA request for policy documents. If you find that material has been released with redactions, you can make an OIA request specifically for the redacted portions, armed with the knowledge of what exists and what was withheld.

Agency Proactive Release Policies and What They Mean for Requesters

Beyond the Cabinet Office requirements, many agencies have developed their own proactive release policies covering a wider range of information. The scope and ambition of these policies vary considerably.

Some agencies have adopted comprehensive policies that cover not only responses to OIA requests but also categories of information that the agency considers to be of public interest: advice to Ministers, briefings to incoming Ministers, ministerial diaries, regulatory decisions, audit reports, research publications, and operational data.

Other agencies have more modest policies, limited to publishing selected OIA responses on their websites after a period following release to the requester. The standard practice in many agencies is to publish OIA responses on the agency's website after a short period (often five working days), with the requester's name and contact details removed.

The Ombudsman's guidance on proactive release emphasises that developing a proactive release culture requires a fundamental shift in how agencies think about information. Rather than treating release as an afterthought or a response to external pressure, agencies should consider publication at the point when information is created. Information that cannot be released should be designed to be easily identifiable, so that redaction is straightforward when the time comes to publish. Agency leaders should send clear and explicit messages to their staff and stakeholders that they encourage and support proactive release.

For requesters, agency proactive release policies are relevant in several ways. Published OIA responses are valuable because they show you not only what information the agency holds but also how it approaches withholding decisions. Reviewing previously published responses can help you craft more effective requests and anticipate the arguments an agency is likely to make.

Proactive release policies also affect the dynamics of the OIA process. Agencies that know their responses will be published may approach withholding decisions differently than they would for a response going only to an individual requester. The knowledge that a response will be publicly visible can cut both ways: it may encourage agencies to be more careful and transparent in their reasoning, but it may also lead to more conservative redaction, particularly where privacy or commercial sensitivity is involved.

Importantly, the existence of a proactive release policy does not replace the OIA. If information has been proactively released with redactions, you can still request the redacted material. If information falls outside the scope of the agency's proactive release policy, you can still request it. Proactive release supplements the OIA; it does not substitute for it.

The FYI Ecosystem: How the Platform Has Changed the OIA Landscape

FYI (fyi.org.nz) is a website that allows anyone to make OIA and LGOIMA requests through an online platform. The key feature of FYI is that all requests and responses are automatically published on the website, creating a searchable public archive of official information.

FYI has changed the OIA landscape in several important ways.

For requesters, FYI provides a simple interface for making requests, a tracking system that records when requests were sent and when responses are due, and automatic publication that creates a permanent, publicly accessible record of both the request and the agency's response. The archive is searchable, which means you can see what other people have asked for, what agencies have released, and how agencies have responded to particular types of requests. This is an invaluable research tool. Before making a request, searching the FYI archive may reveal that someone else has already asked for the same or similar information, saving you the effort of a duplicate request.

For the broader public, FYI has created a form of crowd-sourced transparency. Every response published on FYI becomes available to everyone, not just the original requester. Over time, the archive has accumulated a substantial body of government information that would otherwise be accessible only to the individuals who originally requested it.

For agencies, FYI has created a new dynamic. Because responses are automatically published, agencies know that their response will be visible to the public, the media, and other agencies. The Ombudsman's guide on requests made online notes that the automatic publication of responses may be relevant to the withholding analysis: on the one hand, it may increase privacy concerns (because information will reach a wider audience than just the requester); on the other hand, it may lend weight to the public interest in disclosure (because the information will become available to the general public).

There are some practical considerations for requesters using FYI. Eligibility can be an issue: to request information under the OIA (as opposed to LGOIMA), you must be a New Zealand citizen, permanent resident, person in New Zealand, or New Zealand-incorporated corporate entity. Agencies that receive requests through FYI have limited information about the requester's identity and eligibility, and may ask you to verify your eligibility. Consider stating your eligibility in the request itself.

Privacy is another consideration. Because all FYI responses are automatically published, any personal information included in the response (your own or others') will become publicly available. If your request is likely to return information that raises privacy concerns, consider making it directly to the agency rather than through FYI, so that the agency can release the information to you without automatic publication.

Some agencies treat FYI requests with greater caution because of the automatic publication feature. This may result in more extensive redactions, longer processing times (due to additional review before publication), or more frequent consultation with third parties. This is not a reason to avoid FYI, but it is something to be aware of.

Finally, the FYI archive is a powerful tool for research and investigation. Before making any OIA request, it is worth searching FYI for previous requests on the same topic. You may find that the information you want has already been released, or that previous responses give you a clearer picture of what the agency holds and how it is likely to approach your request.

Open Data and the Shift Towards Publishing Information by Default

Alongside proactive release of documents, there has been a parallel movement towards making government data available in open, reusable formats. This is the open data agenda, and it operates at the intersection of transparency policy, technology, and the OIA.

Under the Declaration on Open and Transparent Government, Cabinet has committed to actively releasing high value public data. The government data portal at data.govt.nz is the central repository for datasets published by government agencies. It hosts thousands of datasets across a wide range of topics: health statistics, education data, environmental monitoring, transport information, crime data, economic indicators, and more.

The New Zealand Government Open Access and Licensing framework (NZGOAL) provides guidance on how agencies should license their data and information for reuse. The goal is to make government data available on open licensing terms wherever possible, so that it can be freely used, shared, and built upon by researchers, journalists, businesses, and the public.

For requesters, the open data movement has several practical implications. The data you need may already be available on data.govt.nz or on an agency's own data portal. Checking these sources before making an OIA request can save significant time and effort.

If you need government data for analysis or research, you can request it in electronic, reusable formats under the OIA. The Act requires agencies to provide information in your preferred format unless doing so would impair efficient administration or prejudice a protected interest. Requesting data in a machine-readable format (such as a spreadsheet or CSV file rather than a PDF) makes it possible to analyse the data effectively, and is consistent with the open data principles that agencies are expected to follow.

The open data movement has not yet reached all parts of government equally. Some agencies have embraced it enthusiastically; others have been slower to publish data or have published it in formats that are difficult to reuse. If you need data that is not available through existing portals, an OIA request remains the appropriate tool.

How Proactive Release Reduces the Need for Individual Requests, and Its Limits

The benefits of proactive release for requesters are real and significant. When agencies publish information proactively, you get it faster (often immediately), without the need for a formal request, without the risk of delay or refusal, and without charges. Proactive release also enables you to discover information you did not know existed, because browsing a website is a different experience from drafting a targeted request.

For the system as a whole, proactive release reduces the volume of individual requests that agencies must process, freeing up resources for the requests that remain. It also improves the quality of the OIA system by shifting energy from reactive processing towards planned, considered publication. The Ombudsman's guidance notes that proactive release allows agencies to become a reliable and authoritative source for their own information, with greater flexibility to decide when and how information is released and what additional context to put around it so that readers can derive greater meaning.

But proactive release has important limits, and requesters should understand these clearly.

Proactive release is voluntary. The OIA does not require agencies to publish information proactively. The Cabinet Office requirements apply only to Cabinet material, and agency proactive release policies are matters of administrative practice rather than legal obligation. An agency that fails to publish information proactively has not breached the OIA.

Proactively released information is curated by the agency. The agency decides what to publish, when to publish it, and what to redact. This means that proactive release is not a substitute for the right to request specific information under the OIA. The information the agency chooses to publish may not be the information you need. The timing of publication may not suit your needs. And the redactions applied to proactively released material may remove precisely the information that matters most to you.

Proactive release does not give you the right to challenge withholding decisions in the way that an OIA request does. If an agency publishes a Cabinet paper with redactions, you cannot complain to the Ombudsman about those redactions unless you make a formal OIA request for the redacted material and the agency refuses. Proactive release operates outside the formal OIA process, and the Ombudsman's jurisdiction is tied to decisions made in response to requests.

There is also a legal difference between proactive release and release in response to an OIA request that is worth noting. Agencies are protected from any civil proceedings (including for breach of copyright) for releasing information in good faith in response to a request made under the OIA or LGOIMA. That statutory protection does not extend to information released proactively. This means agencies must conduct a more careful legal review before publishing information proactively, which can affect both the speed and the scope of what is published.

The quality of proactive release varies enormously between agencies. Some agencies publish material in well-organised, searchable repositories with clear metadata and open licensing. Others publish documents in poorly labelled files buried deep in their website structure, with no search function and no clear system of organisation. The utility of proactively released information depends not just on its existence but on its accessibility and discoverability.

Finally, proactive release covers only some of the information that agencies hold. Even the most ambitious proactive release policy will not cover internal correspondence, operational files, contractual documents, personnel records, legal advice, or the vast volume of routine administrative information that agencies accumulate in the course of their work. For this material, the OIA remains the only route of access.

For requesters, the practical conclusion is straightforward. Use proactive release as a starting point, not an endpoint. Check agency websites, the FYI archive, data.govt.nz, and other public sources before making a request. Use what you find to inform and sharpen your OIA requests. But do not assume that proactive release gives you everything you need. The OIA exists precisely for the information that agencies do not publish voluntarily, and your right to request it is unaffected by the growth of proactive release.

The Danks Committee envisaged a system in which the availability of official information would increase progressively over time. Proactive release is the most visible manifestation of that vision. Former Chief Ombudsman Sir Brian Elwood expressed the hope that more information would be released into the public domain as a matter of course, without the need to make a formal request for it. That hope is being realised, unevenly and incompletely, but in a direction that serves the purposes of the Act. As a requester, you benefit from this trend. But the OIA remains your ultimate safeguard, and the right to request information that the government has not chosen to publish remains as important as it has ever been.

APPENDICES

Appendix A — Comparative Table of Provisions

OIA = Official Information Act 1982 (as at 5 April 2025)
LGOIMA = Local Government Official Information and Meetings Act **1987** (as at 15 January 2026)
PA = Privacy Act 2020 (as at 27 November 2025)
NCND = neither confirm nor deny
PI = public interest
LA = local authority
HRRT = Human Rights Review Tribunal
IPP = information privacy principle.

Table 1 — General Provisions

This table maps corresponding provisions across the three Acts. 'N/A' indicates no equivalent provision. References to the Privacy Act ('PA') are to the Privacy Act 2020.

Subject	OIA	LGOIMA	PA 2020
PRELIMINARY			
Interpretation	s 2	s 2	s 7
'Official information' defined	s 2(1)	s 2(1)	N/A
'Personal information' defined	s 2(1)	s 2(1)	s 7(1)
'Document' defined	s 2(1)	s 2(1)	s 7(1)
'Working day' defined	s 2(1)	s 2(1)	s 7(1)

Eligibility to request	s 12(1): NZ citizens, perm residents, persons in NZ, NZ bodies corporate	s 10(1): any person	IPP 6: individual concerned or representati ve
Info held by officers/employees	s 2(3)	s 2(3)	s 10
Info held by contractors	s 2(5)	s 2(6)	s 11
Bodies not covered	s 2(6): courts, tribunals (judicial), Royal Commissions, etc.	N/A (Sch 1 defines)	s 8(b): Sovereign, Parliament, Ombudsm en, news entities, etc.
Act binds Crown	s 3	s 3	s 6
Purposes	s 4	s 4	s 3

AVAILABILITY & ACCESS RIGHTS

Principle of availability	s 5	s 5	N/A (IPP 6 provides access right)
Access to personal info (natural persons)	s 12(1A) → PA	s 10(1A) → PA	IPP 6; Part 4
Access to personal info (bodies corporate)	s 24 (Part 4)	s 23 (Part 4)	N/A
Access to internal rules	s 22	s 21	N/A
Right to reasons for decisions	s 23	s 22	N/A

MAKING & HANDLING REQUESTS

Making a request	s 12	s 10	IPP 6; s 40
Form of request (any, incl oral)	s 12(1AA)	s 10(1AA)	N/A

Due particularity	s 12(2)	s 10(2)	N/A
Urgency	s 12(3)	s 10(3)	s 41
Oral request — clarification	s 12(4)–(5)	s 10(4)–(5)	N/A
Duty to assist	s 13	s 11	s 42
Transfer (10 working days)	s 14	s 12	s 43
Decision (20 working days)	s 15(1)	s 13(1)	s 44(1)
Amended request = new request	s 15(1AA)–(1AB)	s 13(7)–(8)	N/A
Extension: large quantity	s 15A(1)(a)	s 14(1)(a)	s 48(1)(a)
Extension: consultations	s 15A(1)(b)	s 14(1)(b)	s 48(1)(b)
Extension: complexity	N/A	N/A	s 48(1)(c)
Charging	s 15(1A)–(2)	s 13(1A)–(3)	s 66

MANNER OF RELEASE

Ways of making info available	s 16(1)	s 15(1)	s 56(1)
Electronic form	s 16(1A)	s 15(1A)	s 56(1)(b)
Requester's preferred way	s 16(2)	s 15(2)	s 56(2)
Reason if not preferred way	s 16(3)	s 15(3)	s 56(3)–(4)
Partial release (deletions)	s 17	s 16	s 55
Conditions on use/disclosure	N/A	N/A	s 54

Table 2 — Withholding & Refusal Grounds

'PI?' indicates whether the public interest override applies. * PA s 53(d) (legal privilege) has no PI override, unlike OIA s 9(2)(h) / LGOIMA s 7(2)(g). '—' indicates no equivalent.

Ground	OIA	LGOIMA	PA 2020	PI?
CONCLUSIVE (NO PUBLIC INTEREST OVERRIDE)				
Security / defence / int'l relations	s 6(a)	s 6(a)	s 51(a)	No

Entrusting by foreign govt	s 6(b)	s 6(b)	s 51(b)	No
Maintenance of law / fair trial	s 6(c)	s 6(c)	s 53(c)	No
Safety of any person	s 6(d)	s 6(d)	s 49(1)(a)(i)	No
Serious damage to economy	s 6(e)	—	—	No
Cook Islands / Niue / Tokelau	s 7	—	s 51(c)–(e)	No

GOOD REASONS (PUBLIC INTEREST OVERRIDE APPLIES)

Privacy of natural persons	s 9(2)(a)	s 7(2)(a)	—	Yes
Trade secrets / commercial position	s 9(2)(b)	s 7(2)(b)	s 52	Yes
Obligation of confidence	s 9(2)(ba)	s 7(2)(c)	—	Yes
Tikanga Maori / waahi tapu	—	s 7(2)(ba)	—	Yes
Health or safety measures	s 9(2)(c)	s 7(2)(d)	—	Yes
Economic interests of NZ	s 9(2)(d)	—	—	Yes
Material loss prevention	s 9(2)(e)	s 7(2)(e)	—	Yes
Constitutional conventions	s 9(2)(f)	—	—	Yes
Free and frank opinions	s 9(2)(g)(i)	s 7(2)(f)(i)	—	Yes
Improper pressure/harassment	s 9(2)(g)(ii)	s 7(2)(f)(ii)	—	Yes
Legal professional privilege	s 9(2)(h)	s 7(2)(g)	s 53(d)	Yes*
Commercial activities	s 9(2)(i)	s 7(2)(h)	—	Yes
Negotiations	s 9(2)(j)	s 7(2)(i)	—	Yes
Improper gain or advantage	s 9(2)(k)	s 7(2)(j)	—	Yes

ADMINISTRATIVE REASONS

Contrary to enactment	s 18(c)(i)	s 17(c)(i)	—	N/A
Contempt of court/House	s 18(c)(ii)	s 17(c)(ii)	s 53(f)	N/A
Soon to be publicly available	s 18(d)	s 17(d)	—	N/A

Criminal Disclosure Act	s 18(da)	s 17(da)	s 53(g)	N/A
Does not exist / cannot be found	s 18(e)	s 17(e)	s 53(a)	N/A
Not readily retrievable	—	—	s 53(aa)	N/A
Substantial collation/research	s 18(f)	s 17(f)	—	N/A
Not held / no reason to believe elsewhere	s 18(g)	s 17(g)	—	N/A
Frivolous / vexatious / trivial	s 18(h)	s 17(h)	s 53(h)	N/A

PERSONAL INFO REFUSAL GROUNDS

Serious threat to life/health/safety	—	—	s 49(1)(a)(i)	No
Serious harassment	—	—	s 49(1)(a)(ii)	No
Victim distress	—	—	s 49(1)(a)(iii)	No
Prejudice health of individual	s 23(2A)(b)	s 22(1A)(b)	s 49(1)(b)	No
Contrary to interests of child <16	s 23(2A)(c)	s 22(1A)(c)	s 49(1)(c)	No
Safe custody / rehabilitation	s 23(2A)(d)	s 22(1A)(d)	s 49(1)(d)	No
Evaluative material	s 27(1)(c)	s 26(1)(c)	s 50	No
Unwarranted disclosure of another	s 27(1)(b)	s 26(1)(b)	s 53(b)	No
Library/museum/archive condition	—	—	s 53(e)	No

Table 3 — Review, Complaints & Other Provisions

This table covers review and complaint mechanisms, personal information access by corporate bodies, miscellaneous provisions, and provisions unique to each Act.

Subject	OIA	LGOIMA	PA 2020

REVIEW & COMPLAINTS

Functions of Ombudsmen / Commissioner	s 28	s 27	ss 69–96
Complaint form	s 28(3): writing or oral	s 27(3): writing or oral	s 72: writing
Review of refusal	s 28(1)(a)	s 27(1)(a)	ss 70–71
Review of manner/charge	s 28(1)(b)	s 27(1)(b)	s 93
Review of conditions	s 28(1)(c)	s 27(1)(c)	N/A
Review of NCND	s 28(1)(d)	s 27(1)(d)	N/A
Review of extension	s 28(2)	s 27(2)	N/A
Deemed refusal (failure to respond)	s 28(4)	s 27(4)	N/A
Undue delay = deemed refusal	s 28(5)	s 27(5)	N/A
Notify Chief Archivist	s 28(6)	s 27(6)	N/A
Ombudsmen Act 1975 applies	s 29	s 28	N/A
20 working day compliance	s 29A	s 29	N/A
Consult Privacy Commissioner	s 29B	s 29A	N/A
Procedure after investigation	s 30	s 30	ss 91–95
PM/AG certificate	s 31	s 31	N/A
Executive override	s 32: Order in Council	s 32: LA resolution	N/A
Override requirements	s 32A	s 33	N/A
Right of review (High Court)	s 32B	s 34	N/A
Appeals (Court of Appeal)	s 32C	s 35	ss 105–108
Inform complainant of result	s 33	s 36	ss 91–94
Must exhaust Ombudsman first	s 34	s 37	N/A

Review of Part 3/4 decisions	s 35	s 38	N/A
Require publication of report	N/A	s 39	N/A

REASON FOR REFUSAL

Reason to be given	s 19	s 18	s 46(2)
Grounds on request	s 19(a)(ii)	s 18(a)(ii)	s 46(3)
Right to complain — notification	s 19(b)	s 18(b)	s 46(2)(b)

PERSONAL INFO (CORPORATE BODIES)

Access right	s 24	s 23	N/A
Restriction to bodies corporate	s 24(2)	s 23(1A)	N/A
Precautions (identity, delivery)	s 25	s 24	s 57
Correction of info	s 26	s 25	IPP 7; ss 58–65
Refusal grounds (Pt 4)	s 27(1)	s 26(1)	ss 49–53
MISCELLANEOUS			
Protection (good faith release)	s 48	s 41	s 205
Exclusion of PI immunity	s 11	s 9	s 209
Savings	s 52	s 44	ss 24, 137
Regulations	s 47	s 55	ss 213–215
Neither confirm nor deny	s 10	s 8	s 47
Substantial collation duties	s 18A	s 17A	N/A
Duty to consult requester	s 18B	s 17B	N/A
Publication of functions	s 20	s 19 [repealed]	N/A
Privacy officers	N/A	N/A	s 201

LGOIMA-SPECIFIC

Land information memoranda	N/A	ss 44A–44D	N/A
Meetings: public notification	N/A	s 46	N/A
Meetings: agendas & reports	N/A	s 46A	N/A
Meetings: public admission	N/A	s 47	N/A
Meetings: exclude public	N/A	s 48	N/A
Meetings: minutes	N/A	s 51	N/A
Delegation by LA	N/A	s 42	N/A
Delegation by officers	N/A	s 43	N/A

PA-SPECIFIC

IPPs 1–13	N/A	N/A	s 22
Codes of practice	N/A	N/A	ss 32–38
Interference with privacy	N/A	N/A	s 69
HRRT proceedings	N/A	N/A	ss 97–111
Access direction	N/A	N/A	s 92
Remedies (damages etc.)	N/A	N/A	ss 102–103
Notifiable privacy breaches	N/A	N/A	ss 112–122
Compliance notices	N/A	N/A	ss 123–135
Information sharing	N/A	N/A	ss 136–161
Information matching	N/A	N/A	ss 174–191
Onward transfer prohibition	N/A	N/A	ss 192–200
Offences	N/A	N/A	s 212

Glossary of Key Terms

This glossary defines the key terms used throughout this book. Where a term has a specific statutory definition, the glossary reflects the statutory language but explains it in plain English. Cross-references to relevant chapters are included where a fuller discussion is available.

Administrative reasons for refusal. The category of refusal grounds found in section 18 of the OIA (section 17 of LGOIMA). Unlike the conclusive reasons (section 6) and good reasons (section 9), administrative reasons are not about protecting a substantive interest. They deal with practical limits on the obligation to provide information: the information is not held, providing it would require substantial collation or research, the information will soon be publicly available, the request is frivolous or vexatious, and so on. Administrative reasons are not subject to the public interest test. However, reliance on them is discretionary, meaning an agency may still choose to release information even if an administrative ground applies. See Chapter 13.

Agency. A body subject to the OIA or LGOIMA. Under the OIA, agencies include government departments, Crown entities, state-owned enterprises, and other organisations listed in the schedules to the Act. Under LGOIMA, agencies include local authorities and council-controlled organisations. Ministers of the Crown are also subject to the OIA in respect of information they hold in their official capacity, but are not usually referred to as "agencies." See Chapter 2.

As soon as reasonably practicable. The standard the OIA sets for the timing of decisions on requests. Section 15(1) requires agencies to make and communicate their decision on a request "as soon as reasonably practicable, and in no case later than 20 working days after the day on which the request is received." The 20-working-day limit is a backstop, not a target. The Ombudsman has emphasised that the primary obligation is to respond as soon as reasonably practicable, which may be well before the 20th working day. See Chapter 8.

Charge. The amount an agency may require a requester to pay for the supply of official information. Agencies have the power to charge a "reasonable" amount. The Government's Charging Guidelines specify what activities can and cannot be charged for, and what rates are appropriate. Decision-making time cannot be charged for. The first half-hour of search and retrieval is free. Charges can be reduced or waived (remitted) on public interest or hardship grounds. Charges are reviewable by the Ombudsman. See Chapter 9.

Charging Guidelines. The guidelines issued by the Ministry of Justice that govern what agencies can charge for supplying official information, the rates that are appropriate, and when charges should be remitted. The full title is *Government Charging Guidelines for OIA Requests*. These guidelines do not have the force of law, but the Ombudsman treats them as the benchmark for assessing whether a charge is reasonable. See Chapter 9.

Collation. In the context of section 18(f) (substantial collation or research), "collation" refers to the process of bringing together information that the agency holds in different places. It is distinguished from "research," which refers to finding the information. Together, these terms describe the physical accessibility of the requested information: how much work is required to locate it and assemble it for release. See Chapter 13.

Conclusive reasons for withholding. The category of withholding grounds found in section 6 of the OIA (and section 6 of LGOIMA). These grounds protect interests considered so important that they are not subject to the public interest test. If a conclusive reason applies, the information must be withheld regardless of any countervailing public interest in release. The conclusive grounds cover: prejudice to security, defence, or international relations; information entrusted in confidence by other governments or international organisations; prejudice to the maintenance of the law; endangering the safety of any person; and (under the OIA only) serious damage to the economy through premature disclosure of economic or financial policy decisions. The threshold is "would be likely to prejudice," meaning a real and substantial risk, not a mere possibility. See Chapter 11.

Consultation with third parties. The process by which an agency seeks the views of people or organisations whose interests may be affected by the release of information. Agencies commonly consult when a request involves personal information about identifiable individuals, commercially sensitive information about businesses, or information provided in confidence. Consultation takes time and is a common reason for extensions. The views of third parties are relevant but not determinative: the decision on release remains the agency's to make. See Chapter 7.

Deemed refusal. When an agency fails to respond to an OIA request within the statutory time limit (20 working days, or a validly extended period), that failure is treated as a refusal for the purposes of the complaint process. This means you can complain to the Ombudsman without waiting for a formal letter of refusal. The concept is established by section 28(4) and (5) of the OIA. See Chapters 8 and 14.

Document. A broad concept under the OIA. "Document" means a document in any form, including any writing on any material; any information recorded or stored by any means (including electronically); any label, marking, or writing that identifies or describes a thing; any book, map, plan, graph, or drawing; and any photograph, film, negative, tape, or other device in which visual images are embodied. The OIA applies to "information" rather than "documents," which is an even broader concept. See Chapter 3.

Due particularity. The requirement in section 12(2) of the OIA that a requester must specify the information they want with sufficient clarity for the agency to identify and locate it. Due particularity does not require legal language, precise document titles, or file references. It simply means the agency must be able to understand what is being asked for. If a request lacks due particularity, the agency has a duty to provide reasonable assistance to help the requester clarify it. Due particularity is not a ground for refusing a request; it is a prerequisite for the request to be valid. See Chapter 5.

Executive override. The mechanism by which the executive can prevent the Ombudsman's recommendation from becoming binding. Under the OIA, this requires an Order in Council (a formal decision of the Governor-General acting on the advice of the Executive Council, which in practice means a Cabinet decision). The Order in Council must be made within 21 working days of the recommendation, must set out reasons and grounds, and must be published in the New Zealand Gazette. Under LGOIMA, the equivalent mechanism is a resolution of the local authority. The override power has not been used since the OIA was amended in 1987 to require collective Cabinet agreement rather than an individual ministerial veto. See Chapter 14.

Extension. The power of an agency to extend the 20-working-day time limit for making a decision on a request. Extensions are permitted only on two grounds: that the request is for, or requires a search through, a large quantity of information and meeting the original time limit would unreasonably interfere with the agency's operations; or that consultations necessary to make a decision cannot reasonably be completed within the original time limit. The extension must be for a "reasonable period," must be notified to the requester within the original 20 working days, and must state the reasons for the extension and the requester's right to complain to the Ombudsman. Only one extension is permitted per request. See Chapter 8.

Free and frank opinions. One of the most commonly invoked withholding grounds, found in section 9(2)(g)(i) of the OIA (section 7(2)(f)(i) of LGOIMA). It protects the free and frank expression of opinions by officers and employees of any agency, or by Ministers, in the course of their duty. To be withheld, the agency must show that withholding is "necessary" to maintain the effective conduct of public affairs through the protection of such opinions. This ground is subject to the public interest test. The Ombudsman has emphasised that there is no presumption that disclosure inhibits candour, that senior officials are expected to be robust, and that factual and background material should not be caught by this ground. See Chapter 12.

Good reasons for withholding. The category of withholding grounds found in section 9 of the OIA (section 7 of LGOIMA). These grounds protect a range of interests including privacy, commercial sensitivity, confidentiality, free and frank opinions, legal professional privilege, negotiations, and others. Unlike the conclusive reasons in section 6, good reasons are subject to the public interest test: even if a good reason for withholding is established, the information must still be released if the public interest in release outweighs the need to withhold. See Chapter 12.

Held. Information is "held" by an agency if it is in the agency's possession or is deemed to be held under the OIA's special provisions. Agencies are deemed to hold information held by their officers, employees, or members in their official capacity (including on personal devices); information held by independent contractors in their capacity as contractors; and information held by unincorporated bodies established to assist or advise the agency. "Held" also means the information must be in existence; there is no obligation to create information to respond to a request (except for statements of reasons under section 23). For undocumented information, "held" means it must be known to people within the agency and able to be recalled. See Chapter 3.

LGOIMA. The Local Government Official Information and Meetings Act 1987. LGOIMA applies to local authorities and council-controlled organisations the same fundamental principles as the OIA applies to central government. The principle of availability, the withholding grounds, and the complaint process are substantially the same, though there are some differences. LGOIMA has no eligibility restrictions (anyone can request information, regardless of citizenship or residence) and includes additional provisions governing public access to local authority meetings. See Chapters 1 and 18.

Neither confirm nor deny. The power in section 10 of the OIA (section 10 of LGOIMA) that allows an agency, in limited circumstances, to refuse to confirm or deny whether information exists. This power may be exercised only if the interest protected by the withholding grounds would itself be prejudiced by confirming or denying the existence of the information. It is a narrow power, used in situations where even acknowledging the existence of information would cause the harm the Act is designed to prevent. See Chapter 10.

No surprises convention. An administrative convention (not a legal rule) under which government departments notify or consult the relevant Minister before releasing information in response to OIA requests that may be politically sensitive or attract media attention. The convention exists to ensure Ministers are not caught unaware by the release of information that may generate public comment or parliamentary questions. Notification is not clearance: the decision on release remains the agency's to make. The convention can add time to the processing of requests and is a common source of delay. See Chapters 7 and 17.

OIA. The Official Information Act 1982. The primary statute governing public access to information held by central government agencies and Ministers of the Crown in New Zealand. See Chapter 1.

Official information. Any information held by an agency or Minister in their official capacity. The definition is extremely broad. It covers documents in any form (paper, electronic, audio, video), emails, text messages, spreadsheets, databases, metadata, and undocumented information known to agency staff and capable of being recalled. Certain categories of information are specifically excluded from the definition: library or museum material held solely for reference or exhibition purposes; information held solely as an agent or for safe custody; evidence or submissions to commissions of inquiry; correspondence with the Ombudsman or Privacy Commissioner in relation to their investigations; victim impact statements; and certain other categories. See Chapter 3.

Ombudsman. An Officer of Parliament, independent of the executive, whose functions include investigating complaints about agency decisions on OIA requests. The Ombudsman can investigate refusals, delays, extensions, charges, the manner of release, and refusals to confirm or deny the existence of information. The Ombudsman's investigation is inquisitorial (the Ombudsman conducts an independent inquiry) and free of charge to the complainant. The Ombudsman's recommendations create a legally binding public duty on the agency to comply, unless the executive override is invoked. The Office of the Ombudsman can be contacted at info@ombudsman.parliament.nz or 0800 802 602. See Chapter 14.

Order in Council. See "Executive override."

Partial release. The release of a document with some information withheld (redacted). Section 17 of the OIA provides that where there is good reason to withhold some of the information in a document, the remaining information may be made available by providing a copy of the document with deletions or alterations as necessary. The agency must give the requester the reason for withholding the redacted information. Partial release is an important feature of the Act: the existence of some sensitive material within a document does not justify withholding the entire document. See Chapters 10 and 16.

Personal information. Any official information held about an identifiable person. Requests by individuals for their own personal information are processed under Part 4 of the OIA (which intersects with the Privacy Act 2020) rather than Part 2. Requests by corporate entities for personal information about themselves are also processed under Part 4. See Chapters 3 and 19.

Principle of availability. The foundational principle of the OIA, set out in section 5. It provides that where the question of whether any official information is to be made available arises under the Act, that question shall be determined in accordance with the purposes of the Act and the principle that the information shall be made available unless there is good reason for withholding it. The principle of availability means that the starting point for every request is release, not withholding. The agency bears the burden of identifying a specific ground in the Act that justifies withholding. See Chapter 1.

Proactive release. The publication of official information by an agency without being asked for it, usually on the internet. Proactive release is not required by the OIA but is consistent with the Act's purpose of progressively increasing the availability of official information. It is encouraged by the Ombudsman and the Public Service Commission. Cabinet Office circulars require proactive release of Cabinet papers and related material. Many agencies also publish OIA responses on their websites. See Chapter 21.

Public interest test. The test applied to withholding grounds under section 9 of the OIA (section 7 of LGOIMA). Even if a good reason for withholding is established, the information must still be released if, in the circumstances of the particular case, the public interest in making the information available outweighs the need to withhold it. Factors that may weigh in favour of release include promoting accountability, enabling informed public participation, facilitating informed debate, correcting misleading information, and supporting the exercise of legal rights. The conclusive reasons in section 6 are not subject to the public interest test. See Chapters 10 and 12.

Reasonable assistance. The duty imposed on agencies by section 13 of the OIA (section 11 of LGOIMA) to give reasonable assistance to a person who wishes to make a request, who has not made a request in accordance with the Act, or who has directed their request to the wrong agency. This duty requires agencies to help requesters formulate their requests clearly and to direct them to the correct agency if necessary. It is a positive obligation, not merely a duty to refrain from obstructing requesters. See Chapter 5.

Redaction. The deletion or obscuring of specific information within a document before it is released. Redaction is the mechanism by which partial release is achieved under section 17 of the OIA. Redacted information is typically shown as blacked-out or whited-out passages in the released document. The agency must identify the withholding ground that applies to each redaction. See Chapters 10 and 16.

Remission. The reduction or waiver of a charge for the supply of official information. Charges may be remitted on two grounds: that the release of the information is in the public interest and should not be inhibited by the imposition of a charge; or that payment of the charge would cause financial hardship to the requester. See Chapter 9.

Request. A request for official information made under section 12 of the OIA (section 10 of LGOIMA). A request can be made orally or in writing, though writing is recommended. The requester does not need to cite the OIA or use legal language. The information sought must be specified with due particularity. See Chapter 5.

Section 22 request. A request under section 22 of the OIA (section 21 of LGOIMA) for access to documents containing policies, principles, rules, or guidelines in accordance with which decisions or recommendations are made in respect of any person or body of persons in their personal capacity. Section 22 provides an enhanced right of access with more limited grounds for refusal than an ordinary OIA request. Notably, the grounds relating to free and frank opinions and legal professional privilege cannot be used to refuse a section 22 request. See Chapter 19.

Section 23 request. A request under section 23 of the OIA (section 22 of LGOIMA) for a written statement of the reasons for a decision or recommendation made about the requester in their personal capacity. The statement must include the findings on material issues of fact, a reference to the information on which those findings were based, and the reasons for the decision. Like section 22, section 23 provides an enhanced right of access with more limited grounds for refusal. See Chapter 19.

Substantial collation or research. A ground for refusing a request under section 18(f) of the OIA (section 17(f) of LGOIMA). It applies where the information requested cannot be made available without substantial collation or research. Before relying on this ground, an agency must genuinely consider three alternatives: charging the requester, extending the time limit, and consulting the requester to see if the request can be narrowed or met in another way. See Chapter 13.

Transfer. The process by which an agency that receives a request for information it does not hold (or that is more closely connected with the functions of another agency) redirects the request to the appropriate agency. Transfers must be made within 10 working days of receiving the request. The agency must also inform the requester that the request has been transferred, to whom, and why. When a request is transferred, the 20-working-day clock restarts at the receiving agency. See Chapter 8.

Undue delay. Delay in making information available after a decision to release has been made. Section 28(5) of the OIA provides that undue delay in making official information available is deemed to be a refusal for the purposes of the complaint process. This means that even after an agency has decided to release information, it must do so promptly, and a requester can complain to the Ombudsman if there is unreasonable delay in the actual release. See Chapter 8.

Withholding grounds. The provisions of the OIA that specify the reasons for which information may be refused. They fall into three categories: conclusive reasons (section 6), good reasons subject to the public interest test (section 9), and administrative reasons (section 18). LGOIMA has equivalent provisions in sections 6, 7, and 17. An agency may refuse a request only on the grounds specified in the Act. There is no general discretion to withhold information for reasons not listed in the statute. See Chapters 10 to 13.

Working day. A day on which the time limits in the OIA run. Under the OIA, a "working day" is any day of the week other than: Saturday and Sunday; Waitangi Day, Good Friday, Easter Monday, Anzac Day, the Sovereign's Birthday, Matariki Observance Day, and Labour Day (and, if Waitangi Day or Anzac Day falls on a Saturday or Sunday, the following Monday); and the period from 25 December to 15 January inclusive. Under LGOIMA, the definition is similar but the Christmas/New Year closedown period runs from 20 December to 10 January, and regional anniversary days are also excluded. When counting working days, day one is the first working day after the day on which the request is received.

Bibliography

Boshier, P. (2022). *Ready or not? A report on the public sector, the OIA, and the pandemic.* Office of the Ombudsman.

Boshier, P. (2025). *The way I see it: Report of Chief Ombudsman Peter Boshier, on leaving Office.* Office of the Ombudsman.

Commission, P. S. (2025). *OIA statistics.* Public Service Commission. https://www.publicservice.govt.nz/guidance/official-information/oia-statistics

Eagles, I., Taggart, M., & Liddell, G. (1992). *Freedom of information in New Zealand.* Oxford University Press.

Education, M. o. (2025). *Guide to Government, Executive and Ministerial Services.* (OIA: 1349918). Ministry of Education

Guide: The OIA and parliamentary privilege. (2019). Office of the Ombudsman Retrieved from https://www.ombudsman.parliament.nz/resources/oia-and-parliamentary-privilege

Official Information Act 1982, New Zealand Legislation (1982). https://www.legislation.govt.nz/act/public/1982/156/en/latest/

The OIA and the public policy making process: A guide to how the OIA applies to information generated in the context of the public policy making process. (2019). Office of the Ombudsman Retrieved from https://www.ombudsman.parliament.nz/resources/oia-and-public-policy-making-process-guide-how-oia-applies-information-generated-context

Ombudsman, O. o. t. (2019a). *Charging: A guide to charging for official information under the OIA and LGOIMA.* Retrieved from https://www.ombudsman.parliament.nz/resources/charging-guide-charging-official-information-under-oia-and-lgoima

Ombudsman, O. o. t. (2019b). *Commercial information: A guide to sections 9(2)(b) and 9(2)(i) of the OIA and sections 7(2)(b) and 7(2)(h) of the LGOIMA.* Retrieved from https://www.ombudsman.parliament.nz/resources/commercial-information-guide-sections-92b-and-92i-oia-and-sections-72b-and-72h-lgoima

Ombudsman, O. o. t. (2019c). *Conclusive reasons for refusing requests: A guide to the conclusive withholding grounds in section 6 of the OIA and LGOIMA.* Retrieved from https://www.ombudsman.parliament.nz/resources/conclusive-reasons-refusing-requests-guide-conclusive-withholding-grounds-section-6-oia

Ombudsman, O. o. t. (2019d). *Confidential advice to government: A guide to section 9(2)(f)(iv) of the OIA.* Retrieved from https://www.ombudsman.parliament.nz/resources/confidential-advice-government-guide-section-92fiv-oia

Ombudsman, O. o. t. (2019e). *Constitutional conventions: A guide to sections 9(2)(f)(i)-(iii) of the OIA.* Retrieved from https://www.ombudsman.parliament.nz/resources/constitutional-conventions-guide-sections-92fi-iii-oia

Ombudsman, O. o. t. (2019f). *Consulting third parties.* Retrieved from https://www.ombudsman.parliament.nz/resources/consulting-third-parties

Ombudsman, O. o. t. (2019g). *Contrary to law and contempt of court or the House: A guide to section 18(c) of the OIA and section 17(c) of the LGOIMA.* Retrieved from https://www.ombudsman.parliament.nz/resources/contrary-law-and-contempt-court-or-house-guide-section-18c-oia-and-section-17c-lgoima

Ombudsman, O. o. t. (2019h). *Dealing with OIA requests involving Ministers: A guide to transfer, consultation, and the notification of decisions on OIA requests.* Retrieved from https://www.ombudsman.parliament.nz/resources/dealing-oia-requests-involving-ministers-guide-transfer-consultation-and-notification

Ombudsman, O. o. t. (2019i). *Free and frank opinions: A guide to section 9(2)(g)(i) of the OIA and section 7(2)(f)(i) of the LGOIMA.* Retrieved from https://www.ombudsman.parliament.nz/resources/free-and-frank-opinions-guide-section-92gi-oia-and-section-72fi-lgoima

Ombudsman, O. o. t. (2019j). *Frivolous, vexatious and trivial: A guide to section 18(h) of the OIA and section 17(h) of the LGOIMA.* Retrieved from https://www.ombudsman.parliament.nz/resources/frivolous-vexatious-and-trivial-guide-section-18h-oia-and-section-17h-lgoima

Ombudsman, O. o. t. (2019k). *Guidance for agencies whose decisions are under investigation by the Ombudsman.* Retrieved from https://www.ombudsman.parliament.nz/resources/guidance-agencies-whose-decisions-are-under-investigation-ombudsman

Ombudsman, O. o. t. (2019l). *Improper gain or advantage: A guide to section 9(2)(k) of the OIA and section 7(2)(j) of the LGOIMA.* Retrieved from https://www.ombudsman.parliament.nz/resources/improper-gain-or-advantage-guide-section-92k-oia-and-section-72j-lgoima

Ombudsman, O. o. t. (2019m). *Improper pressure or harassment: A guide to section 9(2)(g)(ii) of the OIA and section 7(2)(f)(ii) of the LGOIMA.* Retrieved from https://www.ombudsman.parliament.nz/resources/improper-pressure-or-harassment-guide-section-92gii-oia-and-section-72fii-lgoima

Ombudsman, O. o. t. (2019n). *Information not held - A guide to sections 18(e) and (g) of the OLA and sections 17(e) and (g) of the LGOIMA.* Retrieved from https://www.ombudsman.parliament.nz/resources/information-not-held-guide-sections-18e-and-g-oia-and-sections-17e-and-g-lgoima

Ombudsman, O. o. t. (2019o). *Legal professional privilege: A guide to section 9(2)(h) of the OLA and section 7(2)(g) of the LGOIMA.* Retrieved from https://www.ombudsman.parliament.nz/resources/legal-professional-privilege-guide-section-92h-oia-and-section-72g-lgoima

Ombudsman, O. o. t. (2019p). *Making official information requests: A guide for requesters.* Retrieved from https://www.ombudsman.parliament.nz/resources/making-official-information-requests-guide-requesters

Ombudsman, O. o. t. (2019q). *Negotiations: A guide to section 9(2)(j) of the OLA and section 7(2)(i) of the LGOIMA.* Retrieved from https://www.ombudsman.parliament.nz/resources/negotiations-guide-section-92j-oia-and-section-72i-lgoima

Ombudsman, O. o. t. (2019r). *The OLA and parliamentary privilege.* Retrieved from https://www.ombudsman.parliament.nz/resources/oia-and-parliamentary-privilege

Ombudsman, O. o. t. (2019s). *The OLA and the public tender process.* Retrieved from https://www.ombudsman.parliament.nz/resources/oia-and-public-tender-process

Ombudsman, O. o. t. (2019t). *An Ombudsman's investigation and review under the OLA or LGOIMA.* Retrieved from https://www.ombudsman.parliament.nz/resources/ombudsmans-investigation-and-review-under-oia-or-lgoima

Ombudsman, O. o. t. (2019u). *Public interest: A guide to the public interest test.* Retrieved from https://www.ombudsman.parliament.nz/resources/public-interest-guide-public-interest-test

Ombudsman, O. o. t. (2019v). *Requests by corporate entities for their personal information: A guide to Part 4 of the OLA and LGOIMA.* Retrieved from https://www.ombudsman.parliament.nz/resources/requests-corporate-entities-their-personal-information-guide-part-4-oia-and-lgoima

Ombudsman, O. o. t. (2019w). *Requests for internal decision making rules: A guide to section 22 of the OLA and section 21 of the LGOIMA.* Retrieved from https://www.ombudsman.parliament.nz/resources/requests-internal-decision-making-rules-guide-section-22-oia-and-section-21-lgoima

Ombudsman, O. o. t. (2019x). *Requests for reasons for a decision or recommendation: A guide to section 23 of the OIA and section 22 of the LGOIMA*. Retrieved from https://www.ombudsman.parliament.nz/resources/requests-reasons-decision-or-recommendation-guide-section-23-oia-and-section-22-lgoima

Ombudsman, O. o. t. (2019y). *Requests made online: A guide to requests made through fyi.org.nz and social media*. Retrieved from https://www.ombudsman.parliament.nz/resources/requests-made-online-guide-requests-made-through-fyiorgnz-and-social-media

Ombudsman, O. o. t. (2019z). *Substantial collation or research: A guide to section 18(f) of the OIA and section 17(f) of the LGOIMA*. Retrieved from https://www.ombudsman.parliament.nz/resources/substantial-collation-or-research-guide-section-18f-oia-and-section-17f-lgoima

Ombudsman, O. o. t. (2020a). *Confidentiality: A guide to section 9(2)(ba) of the OIA and section 7(2)(c) of the LGOIMA*. Retrieved from https://www.ombudsman.parliament.nz/resources/confidentiality-guide-section-92ba-oia-and-section-72c-lgoima

Ombudsman, O. o. t. (2020b). *Names and contact details of public sector employees*. Retrieved from https://www.ombudsman.parliament.nz/resources/names-and-contact-details-public-sector-employees

Ombudsman, O. o. t. (2020c). *Privacy: A guide to section 9(2)(a) of the OIA and section 7(2)(a) of the LGOIMA*. Retrieved from https://www.ombudsman.parliament.nz/resources/privacy-guide-section-92a-oia-and-section-72a-lgoima

Ombudsman, O. o. t. (2020d). *Proactive release: Good practices for proactive release of official information*. Retrieved from https://www.ombudsman.parliament.nz/resources/proactive-release-good-practices-proactive-release-official-information

Ombudsmen Act 1975, New Zealand Legislation (1975). https://legislation.govt.nz/act/public/1975/9/en/latest

Price, S., & New Zealand Centre for Public, L. (2005). *The Official Information Act 1982 : a window on government or curtains drawn?*

Privacy Act 2020, New Zealand Legislation (2020). https://www.legislation.govt.nz/act/public/2020/31/en/latest/

Taylor, G. D. S., & Roth, P. (2017). *Access to information* (Second edition. ed.). LexisNexis NZ Limited.

Wakem, B. (2015). *Not a game of hide and seek : report on an investigation into the practices adopted by central government agencies for the purpose of compliance with the Official Information Act 1982*. Office of the Ombudsman.

White, N., & Victoria University of Wellington. Institute of Policy, S. (2007). *Free and frank : making the New Zealand Official Information Act 1982 work better*. Institute of Policy Studies.